JOHN
LENNON
& THE FBI FILES

Printed and bound in Great Britain by Butler & Tanner Ltd, Frome, Somerset

Published by Sanctuary Publishing Limited, Sanctuary House, 45–53 Sinclair Road, London W14 0NS, United Kingdom

www.sanctuarypublishing.com

ISBN: 1-86074-522-9

JOHN LENNON

& THE FBI FILES

Phil Strongman & Alan Parker

Sanctuary

Contents

Acknowledgements

Alan and Phil would like to thank
Mr and Mrs H Parker, David Parker, Harry and Do-Do, Masuko, Vince and Christo, Jay and JD, Robert Kirby at PFD, Jonathan Richards, Sean at Helter Skelter, Rob Lythall at VIP, Sam Davies, Chuck Taylor and all the NYPD guys, Steve Woof at EMI, Edward Christie, Rav Singh (the 5th Beatle), Everyone at the UK Beatles Fan Club, Gary at From Me To You, Mick O'Shea, Paul and Graham at the Cinema Store, James, Dave and Lucy at Creation, Mr Sil Willcox, Jack and Andy at *Record Collector*, Paul Wayne at Tracks, Melissa Palmer (Alan's Wee Me), Iain MacGregor, Chris Harvey and Laura Brudenell, and everyone on planet Stiff Little Fingers.

Special thanks to
May Pang, Roy Carr, Bob Gruen and Bill Harry who uncomplainingly answered questions about happenings long ago and worlds apart.

Introduction

Alan Parker came up with the idea for this book and contributed a lot of the research; that's when he wasn't drinking – or romancing gangsters' molls and table dancers. He was also busy scribbling two other books at the time – on Stiff Little Fingers songs and Clash discographies – so I ended up doing most of the writing. Therefore, if you hate the following it's probably only fair to say it's slightly more my fault than his.

As to the book itself I have to say from the off that it probably wouldn't have happened at all unless Lennon scholar and history professor Jon Wiener hadn't first prised the FBI files open (and his *Gimme Some Truth* remains the definitive book about trying to bring the superstate to account). Similarly Fenton Bresler, the British lawyer who first asked awkward questions about John's assassination, deserves all our thanks for this – and for his *Who Killed John Lennon?* book.

This, our own effort, is not meant to be yet another Beatles book nor is it, in the main, about John Lennon's music. Roy Carr, Hunter Davies, Ray Coleman and Iain MacDonald have made all such efforts pretty surplus to requirements. Although there is the odd revelation, and a spot of myth-debunking here and there, this tome is mainly about the FBI's persecution of Lennon and what led to it, in both cultural and political terms (as well as what came of it). We've also tried to show the connections – some obvious, some almost invisible – between him and some of the biggest events and most famous names of the 20th century: Kennedy, Luther King, Nixon, Reagan, Bush and Blair.

It may seem to some that they're pretty big names for a guitar-playing singer/songwriter from Liverpool to be amongst but many of us too often underplay the power of music. We forget that Irish war drums were banned for centuries, that Tchaikovsky's music was thought to have bewitched the Russian Tsarina as much as Rasputin and, even in the staid classical theatres of the 1920s, new works by Ravel and Prokofiev provoked riots among their well-heeled followers. The beat groups, like rock 'n' rollers before them and punks afterwards, caused angry newspaper editorials, raised questions in parliament and changed many of the leading lights of several generations – for better *and* worse. We forget too that, following John Lennon's death, there were memorial gatherings that were, in total, millions strong. Millions more joined in a ten-minute worldwide silent vigil.

Popular music has power, generates big money, has to be controlled. These are simple but true facts. Right into my lifetime, right up until the early '80s, popular music shows on British television lasted for just over one hour a week. That was it. The limit. Live music – even a single guitarist – was licensed like a dog in Britain (and still is, in fact the current regime is trying to make the laws even stricter).

But recorded music is everywhere now, like the air we breathe, and, like the air we depend on, it's easy to take it all for granted. I know I took John Lennon and The Beatles for granted – right up until that foggy day I staggered off a train in London and the TV screens in all the shops showed only one image: John Lennon. A sinking feeling in the pit of my stomach instantly told me that the news about Lennon was the worst it could be. Rock stars only led the news by their death in those days.

Millions of us suffered a little death on 8 December 1980 – The Beatles had been part of our childhood, our adolescence, our youth, our lives. According to tabloid reporters, only Princess Diana's death matched Lennon's for impact. To almost every young man and woman The Beatles were once 'everyman', just like him next door and that lad over the road. They knew us, we knew them. A smile, a wink, a song. Except that The Beatles were just that bit more talented, that touch more amusing and though age and honesty later revealed their faults we still loved them then. And we love them still.

Lennon was the sarcastic leader who was also the idealistic dreamer; the angry poet who was also the passionate lover; the man who stripped naked for love and went to bed for world peace was also the absent husband; the one-night stand merchant was also the repentant father; the last serious Jack the Lad was also the first male feminist. John Lennon was also, most shockingly, the first Beatle to die, as should have been obvious to all of us from the start...

At the time of Lennon's killing, Reagan and the men behind him were busy trying to hot up the Cold War, while I was busy trying to make a short film – long since abandoned – about the not-so-accidental death of a rock star. I didn't get the blatant connection with what had just happened in New York. I didn't even notice the Hanratty connection – the real-life miscarriage of justice case was to be featured in the short film and screenplay that I later wrote about it. All without knowing, or remembering, John and Yoko's own, far more famous, attempt to help the Hanrattys. It was probably just sheer ignorance on my part, but I'd like to think it was an 'age thing' as well: you just don't see the 'connectedness' of everything when you're younger. It takes time to make sense of it all.

The bigger, clearer picture – the *vision* – was something that John Lennon had acquired by the time of his death. It was an international vision, and one that some people feared. Including members of America's intelligence agencies...

We started this unsure of where it would all lead. Surely the FBI had revealed all its Lennon files? Surely the police investigation into this death had been thorough? Surely there were no strong links to those other shocking assassinations of the recent past? Surely there were no links to religious fanatics, the other US killings, the CIA? Surely not? Surely...?

The following, then, is an account of Lennon's American life – up to and including the last Bermuda and Record Plant sessions – and his abrupt death, in particular the role of the FBI and others in trying to break and deport him from the US. He wasn't broken and he didn't leave. Now he's gone. Gone forever...but there still remains the music and the dreams and all those other things that files – or bullets – cannot kill...

Phil Strongman, August 2003

1 Pay To The Order Of

'**Death of A Hero**... The Beatles were more than mere pop minstrels
– and John Lennon was much more than just their leader.'
– Daily Mirror *editorial, London, 9 December 1980*

'I'll outlive the bastards, in more ways than one.'
– *John Lennon*

1-2-3-4!
8 December 1980. The soft-faced stranger dropped into a three-point
combat stance – both hands on the gun – and blasted away. The first
four gunshots hit their target dead-on, in a cluster. Each bullet's hollow
point exploding with catastrophic force within the victim's body. The
Geneva Convention bans hollow point, or dum-dum, bullets for just this
reason, for the sheer amount of horrendous damage they inflict on the
human body...

The sound of a fifth shot then echoed thunderously around the
entrance to the exclusive Dakota Building. The victim's companion slipped
down into a protective crouch near the driveway gates. The companion
was the victim's wife and she'd been a schoolgirl in wartime Tokyo
decades before. Each night, fleets of American B-29 bombers had taken
off from Hawaii, refuelled in the mid-Pacific and then brought death to
the capital of Imperial Japan.

After the warning sirens sounded, the young Yoko Ono would huddle
in the family basement, listening to the muffled thump of man-made
thunder as it drew closer and closer. She once, many years later, likened
the approaching bombs to the footsteps of giants. Hour after hour she
would sit in the dark shivering, waiting for the *gai-jin*, waiting for the

American colossus to stomp on her family's ageing wooden house, waiting for it to snuff out her young life.

In a way, it was a trauma that was to continue to haunt her, a persistent, if tiny, nagging doubt that was always at the back of the brain. *When would they strike? When would they strike...?*

1-2-3-4!

John Lennon was the victim that December night. The singer/songwriter was the product of a failed dockside marriage between a sailor and a showgirl.

Although his father was working class, Lennon was mostly raised in the middle-class suburbia of his Aunt Mimi – which made him, in British terms, a class mutation. 'Semi working class', 'progressive working class' or 'lower-lower middle class'. In other words, an outsider.

His mother had returned in his teens, to bewitch him with her music and to finally befriend him – before she died young under the wheels of 'a drunk-driving cop'. Apart from one traumatic weekend, his father didn't return at all. Not until it no longer counted.

The child Lennon doodled and sketched, created his own magazines and poems, got along with most kids but showed a temper that could be extremely fierce.

Consequently, the driven teenage Lennon got into endless scrapes and left school at 15, virtually without qualifications. But he blagged his way into art school and then, as on a whim, he started The Quarrymen, a skiffle group that also played some rock 'n' roll – the Elvis-led pheno-menon that had convulsed the world of youth since going worldwide in 1956. Lennon once said that, before Elvis Presley, there was nothing that really moved him. Although age brought perspective, for the rest of his life Lennon was to be in thrall, at least partly, to the power of rock 'n' roll – to him it represented communication that was both lyrical and musical, general and specific, street smart and cleverly instinctive.

The Quarrymen attracted Paul McCartney – a happy-go-lucky young rocker whose easy smile hid the fact that he, like Lennon, was also mourning a dead mother. Over the next couple of years, mainly at Lennon's instigation, they transformed themselves into the greatest songwriting duo in musical history – and The Quarrymen added McCartney's friend George Harrison to the line-up and became The Beatles, a rock 'n' roll group.

At the beginning of the '60s The Beatles thought that songs were 'free, like the air' and they themselves played for just food money in the bars, strip-joints and brothels of Liverpool and Hamburg.

By the middle of the '60s The Beatles were the '60s – their self-penned records at Number One, Two, Three, Four and Five in the US and Australian charts, their albums selling millions in the UK, Europe and Japan, their fashions, hairstyles and attitude copied worldwide by every other person under 30, their fame finally eclipsing the technicolour Elvis Presley who'd originally inspired them.

It was the cheeky, charming, arrogant Lennon who had founded The Beatles. And it was he who led them from the crummiest of paint-peeling dives to the brushed velvet of royal performances. On world tours he led them through a cigar haze of VIPs and wheelchairs groaning with the handicapped – there to be 'cured' by superstar fame – and on into outdoor arenas bristling with Kleig lights, TV cameras and tens of thousands of hysterical fans. He led them onto live telecasts seen by over 400 million people across five continents.

For The Beatles were the first band to write virtually all their own material, the first band to use pop videos, the first band to use feedback on record, the first band to use – and be the subject of – pop cartoons, the first band to notch up three hit feature films, the first band to achieve simultaneous hits in dozens of countries. They revived and enhanced the role of the electric guitar. Their covers, and their originals, effectively broke motown – and thus soul music – in the UK and US, and then across the world. Then they helped to do the same for Jamaican reggae and Indian sitar music.

In Poland, East Germany, Czechoslovakia and Russia they were heroes to those who despised Soviet communism, in Latin America they appealed to those opposed to US imperialism and conservative Roman Catholicism. In Japan they caused riots by finally opening the sacred martial arts venue, the Nippon Budokan Hall, to popular music (and they needed over 3,000 cops to protect them from both girl fans and from angry middle-aged reactionaries). In the Philippines a half-hearted snub to dictator's wife Imelda Marcos led to physical attacks by 200 Marcos cronies at a desperate airport getaway.

Everywhere they went, headlines and flashbulbs, screaming limos and screaming fans. Bigger than Cliff Richard! Bigger than Elvis Presley! Bigger than Jesus…?

By then The Beatles, the Fab Four, had managed, quite simply, to conquer the world – without bile or bloodshed, but purely by dint of their own songs, jokes, books, films and cartoons – opening the way for many others as they went. They larked their way to the very top and, despite massive and growing pressure, they made it seem effortless – as casual as their clothes became, for all Paul McCartney's musical and lyrical genius, for all of George Harrison's poetic flourishes, for all of Ringo's good-fellow strength, for all George Martin's technical brilliance and for all Brian Epstein's suave hustling…none of it, none of it, not one bit would have happened without John Winston Lennon.

No 'Please Please Me', no 'I Want To Hold Your Hand', no 'A Hard Day's Night', no 'Ticket To Ride', no 'Help!', no 'Day Tripper', no 'Lady Madonna', no 'Revolution', no 'Don't Let Me Down', no 'Come Together', no 'Strawberry Fields', no 'Rain', no 'Sergeant Pepper', no 'Norwegian Wood', no 'Nowhere Man', no 'Day In The Life', no 'All You Need Is Love'.

Add to that, or rather take away, no hippies, no glam rockers, no punks, no slackers, no ravers, no Live Aid, no 'We Are The World'. no Stones, no Who, no Kinks, no Small Faces, no Byrds, no electric Dylan, no Monkees, no Hendrix, no Led Zeppelin, no Fleetwood Mac, no Rod Stewart, no Bowie, no Roxy Music, no Elton John, no Bee Gees, no Chic, no Sex Pistols, no Clash, no U2, no Nirvana, no White Stripes, no Glastonbury, no '60s, no Oasis. None of it.

By the end of the '60s he was John Winston Ono Lennon, husband of Yoko Ono, Japan's leading avant-garde artist, and The Beatles were falling apart, seemingly burnt-out multi-millionaires with their cash caught between managers and lawyers, pop veterans who had already sold well over 630 million recordings – one for every single family on the planet they had discreetly changed forever.

That much influence, that much power, cannot but help be political in some sense of the word. Both Lennon and McCartney were aware of this dimension to their work and its impact – it was something they took turns to ignore, to flirt with and, occasionally, to confront.

But it was Lennon who took things further, a superstar who took his place on the streets alongside students and workers on marches and demos, it was Lennon who spent tens of thousands of his own dollars on anti-war campaigns.

1-2-3-4!

Just under four minutes after the shooting the cops arrived at the Dakota. The Dakota is the building of which movie star Richard Burton once said that anyone who moves into it must think there's 'someone after them' because it's built like a fortress. It is situated in Manhattan, in the heart of the New York that Lennon loved.

The Dakota is also a building with a forbidding gothic exterior – something that made it a cert as the setting for Roman Polanski's 1968 occult horror flick *Rosemary's Baby*. That was the same year The Beatles had stayed at the Maharishi's retreat in Rishikeh, India, along with their wives, and celebs like Mia Farrow and her shy sister Prudence (for whom John had written 'Dear Prudence' in an attempt to make her smile).

Rosemary's Baby had actually starred Mia Farrow – a Manhattan resident who strolled past the Dakota every other day in 1980, including 8 December – and it was a film with a dark postscript for both its director and Lennon's Beatles.

In the Summer of 1969 Polanski's wife Sharon Tate was butchered by the Charles Manson gang in Los Angeles – a killing some claimed was inspired by *Rosemary's Baby*, a killing Manson himself said was sparked off by The Beatles' songs 'Helter Skelter' and 'Piggies', a killing others mistakenly thought was the first fatal celebrity stalking (it wasn't – Hollywood starlet Sharon Tate hadn't actually been the intended target that night, the gang had really gone there to kill the absent owner, Terry Melcher, a music producer who'd failed to advance the rock career of Manson, an alleged auditionee for US television's own Beatles, The Monkees pop group...).

Even as the flower children partied at Woodstock, in the foothills above LA, Manson's knife groupies were hammering a bloody full stop onto the end of the '60s – the decade The Beatles had made their own. It was a dark omen, and a grim end to the last great golden age of optimism, the last real decade of hope...

As the cops pulled up outside the Dakota that December night, their sirens wailing like mad babies, Lennon lay dying inside, tended by Yoko. The '80s, a decade he might yet have galvanised, had barely begun – and a few dozen feet away his assassin was quietly hanging about, blankly waiting to be arrested.

The killer, one Mark David Chapman, could easily have gotten away – no one was holding him and the Dakota is a mere stone's throw from both Central Park and New York's subway system. There are also several major roads nearby, all regularly served by cabs and buses. A disabled senior citizen could have limped out of sight in under 30 seconds. And Chapman had almost four minutes – why hadn't he run away? Why hadn't he at least tried?

These were questions that must have occurred to Lieutenant Arthur O'Connor, the detective CO of New York's 20th precinct, as he studied Chapman in his cell later that night.

1-2-3-4!

The Fab Four had been close to their official death when John Lennon had touched down, for the last time, on American soil nine years previously. He'd arrived on the run from fading Beatlemania and the cold shoulder that Britain, and 'his' band, had casually shown his exotic new wife.

The couple had flown over to New York in pursuit of Yoko's daughter Kyoko, illegally snatched by her blood-father Anthony Cox. John and Yoko were themselves then plunged into a heavy-duty immigration battle with the US authorities – namely the Immigration and Naturalization Service (INS), which was acting hand in glove with the Federal Bureau of Investigations (FBI) and the Central Intelligence Agency (CIA), all at the behest of the government of a right-wing Republican President, one Richard Milhouse Nixon.

1-2-3-4!

The reason, officially, that Nixon tried to get Lennon deported was because of a four-year-old drug bust – a small amount of cannabis had allegedly been found in a London flat Lennon had been staying in during 1968. That was the stated reason. But everyone in New York knew it was really because Lennon had associated with radicals and had supported the anti-Vietnam War – and thus anti-Nixon – faction with both his time and money. Lennon's political views were his own and in the United States of America he was allowed to enjoy, technically at least, freedom of speech. This is something that is protected by America's First Amendment. But some free speech is 'freer' than others – Lennon's views were to cost him plenty.

When Lennon claimed the US authorities were bugging his phones and following his every move he was accused of paranoia – and when he told friends that if anything happens to 'me or Yoko it won't be an accident', the paranoia jibe seemed justified.

Most people would have given up trying to settle in New York anyway at that point, but the couple had warmed to the city's mood and energy and decided that they wanted to stay there, and besides, John Lennon wasn't most people.

He and Yoko fought the deportation every step of the way – whilst still talking, and marching, against the war. They spent tens of thousands of dollars on lawyers' fees, they won over the city's mayor and most of the city's artists, they lost every round but they always won minor extensions and they always appealed. Eventually the pressure became unbearable – they quarrelled and separated and then, 15 months later, they reunited.

In May 1972 the FBI director, J Edgar Hoover, died, in 1973 Yoko Ono was grudgingly granted the right to stay in the USA, and in 1974 President Nixon resigned rather than face impeachment over the Watergate scandal. Within two years Lennon himself was granted his own green card. He had finally won the right to live and work legally in New York City, indefinitely. Whereupon he promptly fell into a four-year-long retirement, becoming a 'househusband' as he helped raise his new son Sean.

1-2-3-4!

Now, in December 1980, Lennon had launched a comeback and he was dominating the magazine covers once again. More importantly, the *Double Fantasy* album he'd made with Yoko was actually a hit on both sides of the Atlantic, as was the trailer single '(Just Like) Starting Over'.

Bob Dylan had more poetry, Michael Jackson more rhythm, Eric Clapton more guitar, David Bowie more style, John Lydon more attitude, Joe Strummer more politics, Elton John more hardcore fans…but John Lennon, for all his faults, was more important than each and every one of them. He was the only musician at that time whose appeal had, almost from point one, breached generations and races, creeds and classes, cultures and continents.

It really didn't matter that Lennon had been away for years and that, in late 1980, the ultra-conservative Ronald Reagan was Republican President-elect – for now there was talk of John Lennon supporting a trades-union strike on the West Coast, of Lennon going on a forthcoming anti-nukes march, of Lennon launching a world tour for his new album, of Lennon issuing a new poetry book, of Lennon revisiting his family in England – there were even rumours around this time of him one day running for political office (well, if a B-movie actor like Ronald Reagan could reach a position of political power, then anything was surely possible). John Lennon was 40 years of age and unashamed – and truly 'starting over'…

Lennon's killer was Mark David Chapman. His family name came from the 13th-century Chapmans, the men who delivered cloth, orders and messages to Britain's cottage-industry weavers. Like Lennon's name it is one that has some Irish connections. This particular Chapman, Mark David, was from Georgia, USA, the Deep South. He was, we were told within hours, a 'schizophrenic', a 'loner', a 'Beatles obsessive' and a 'manic autograph hunter'.

More importantly he was, we were assured, a 'lone nut' – just like all those other assassins of recent American history, Lee Harvey Oswald, James Earl Ray, Sirhan Sirhan…Chapman was a 'half crazy' fan of John Lennon – 'Lennon's Biggest Fan!' – a stalker who would do almost anything to be famous.

A few days before, he had flown in from Hawaii – just like the wartime B-29s – the blue-eyed 'colossus' Yoko Ono may well have feared for most of her adult life. Except this pudgy-faced youth was no colossus – nor was he a big John Lennon fan, nor was he a Beatles fan, nor was he an autograph hunter, nor was he crazy, nor yet was he a loner...

It was to be another nine years before British lawyer Fenton Bresler casually led Lieutenant O'Connor to the disturbing admission that, on the night of 8 December 1980, Mark David Chapman behaved as if he might well have been in a trance, as if he could have been, quote, 'programmed'...

And it was to be almost another nine years before history professor Jon Wiener finally forced the FBI to begin releasing the bulk of its files on the 'dangerous extremist' they knew as 'John Winston Lennon SM-REVACT 100-469910'; in English these acronyms meant that Lennon had been filed under 'Security Matters, Revolutionary Activities'...

The man who'd founded the lovable moptop Beatles had actually been classified as a serious threat to the security of the continental US – his every move to be watched and recorded and then forwarded to a range of recipients that included the FBI directorate, the White House, the CIA, the DIA, US Naval Intelligence...

John Lennon's death brought all of this official – and often illegal – skullduggery sharply into focus.

In Lennon's death, like his life, are all those elemental strands that continue to dominate the news today – the cult of celebrity, the distance between artist and audience, the infiltration of both the total free market and the intelligence networks into the arts and media, the rise and fall of the Cold War, the rise and rise of US power – and the public's right to know how, when and why their governments have failed to 'give 'em some truth'...

1-2-3-4!

As with all major artists, part of what made John Lennon great was his ability to articulate, and communicate, the deepest thoughts and emotions of millions. Perhaps part of that appeal was the fact that Lennon, beneath the hard-as-nails front, was vulnerable, a war baby, born in 1940. And in telling of his own little war with the FBI – what led up to it and what, shockingly, came of it – in many ways we also tell our own story – and that of millions of other Cold War babies who were always only four minutes away from oblivion...

2 Roots

'The child until seven years of age is father to the man.'
— *Jesuit saying*

The FBI began in 1908 as the United States' need for a police force that operated across state and county lines. President Theodore 'Teddy' Roosevelt had originally wanted the FBI – then still within the Justice Department – to be a force that would fight western landgrabbers and the big East Coast business trusts. Two difficult but undeniably noble tasks.

But, in 1915, the FBI changed direction and was enlarged, when a panicking President Wilson saw the continuing influx of immigrants as being a tide that would bring in a flotsam of wildcat strikers and bomb-throwing anarchists – all the trouble and chaos of the decadent 'Old World' of Europe.

There were two other main reasons for this FBI expansion – Europe itself had been at war since the previous summer and there had also been a growing number of labour disputes in the United States (this latter factor was perhaps inevitable – there were no more major goldrushes after the turn of the century and most of the choice American farmland had already been grabbed decades before; newcomers without private wealth had no choice but to congregate in the cities or industrial towns, and fight for basic wages and conditions – for such new arrivals the saying 'Here or nowhere is your America' was a living motto, not simply some poetic abstraction).

The US entered the First World War in 1917, sealing the fate of Germany and her crumbling Austro-Hungarian ally. The 1918 Armistice allowed the beaten German army to march home with flags flying (a big mistake, since it propagated the myth, later exploited by Hitler, that Germany's troops had not been defeated in battle but, instead, cheated by civilians). The subsequent Treaty of Versailles was, by contrast, overly strict and later forced Germany into hyper-inflation and near-bankruptcy.

This only created resentment as well as depriving both the US and Britain of a once-valuable export market. The labour disputes that then racked the UK – epitomised by the 1926 General Strike – were not echoed to quite the same extent on the other side of the Atlantic, despite much Stateside picket line violence, usually engineered by local police, employer's security guards...and the FBI. Although the US is a vast nation, there was another factor beyond geography that prevented industrial disputes spreading nationwide – the wealth of Wall Street, where a huge boom in stocks and shares seemed to promise eventual dividends for almost everyone.

By 1934 the pug-faced J Edgar Hoover had taken over complete control of the FBI as the Bureau's new director – the seemingly straight-laced 39 year old then faced a massive task. The shares boom had ended with the Wall Street Crash of 1929, and the following worldwide recession sent crime rates spiralling, particularly in the US.

Gun-toting gangs like those run by Dillinger and Bonnie and Clyde were shooting up midwestern banks on a daily basis, while cities like Chicago and New Orleans were increasingly dominated by the organised crime mobs who'd boomed during America's 13-year prohibition on alcohol consumption.

The fact that some of the gunmen occasionally spread a little of their largesse around gave them a Robin Hood appeal to sections of the new jobless – and often homeless – masses (the latter believed, rightly, that the free-market Republican government of Herbert Hoover (no relation to J Edgar) had done absolutely nothing for them during its 1929–33 term of office).

Both the Dillinger and Clyde Barrow gangs were smashed – their leaders, including Ms Bonnie Parker, dying in a hail of bullets as the myth of the FBI's unstoppable 'g-men' was born.

Yet the gangsters' Robin Hood image continued to be played up by Hollywood in endless B-movies that, despite their moralistic endings –

usually featuring Hoover's neatly suited 'g-men' – almost always glamorised the criminals they were supposedly condemning ('Don't do it like this, kids!').

Hollywood also represented one of only two American industries that would tolerate leftism, unseen homosexuality, racial mixing – in private – and the discreet use of soft drugs. The only other industry that would, in a moralistic yet racially segregated nation, stand for such 'excesses' was the music industry, then built around big bands, live radio and the jukebox circuits, some of which were mob-dominated.

The organised-crime element, despite its violence and its infiltration of some entertainment labour unions, didn't worry Hoover at all – he continued, after all, to deny the very existence of organised crime, a claim he maintained right up until the '60s. What worried Hoover far more were 'moral' and 'political' transgressions, especially amongst entertainers, those who might speak out on the big issues of the day, those who might have some 'undue' influence on the general public.

When it came to 'moral' and 'political' mistakes, to Hoover the former meant marijuana or extra-marital sex and the latter meant any kind of support for socialism or left-leaning liberalism. In this, Hoover was both hypocritical and himself a law breaker. The FBI was not supposed to discourage any kind of free speech – it was, and is, protected by the US Constitution – and when it came to puritanical morality, J Edgar Hoover the FBI's boss for almost three decades, was himself a homosexual transvestite who, like his lifelong close 'companion' Clyde Tolson, was not above using blackmail to force vulnerable young men into bed.

Despite these secret incongruities, Hoover's Bureau had grown into a force tens of thousands strong by the late '30s. By then the New Deal of liberal Democrat President Franklin D Roosevelt had slowed and, in some areas, even reversed the rise in crime.

Which freed Hoover to concentrate on his obsessions – he spent millions of dollars on phone taps, surveillance photos, 'tails', gossip columnists and informers, as a vast array of files was constructed. Whenever a politician, an actor, a singer or a trades-union leader committed any kind of 'moral outrage', it was noted by the FBI, the evidence carefully filed away for future use…

By September 1939, the ugly seeds planted at Versailles had started to bloom. Hitler's Nazi Germany – having already helped Franco destroy Spanish democracy – attacked its eastern neighbour Poland. The resulting Second World War brought heavy bombing to northern Britain for the very first time.

According to legend, on the night of 9 October 1940, the northwestern seaport of Liverpool was subjected to a particularly heavy raid. The Oxford Street Maternity Hospital was shaken but suffered no direct hits. To celebrate her newborn son's survival of the bombing, Julia Lennon gave him the middle name 'Winston' – in honour of Britain's leader, Winston Churchill.

The actual truth is, however, a little different – there were no bombing raids, heavy or otherwise, on Liverpool between 7 and 10 October. The child's middle name was simply a product of the widespread belief, justified as it turned out, that the new prime minister was the right man to prevent a Nazi invasion. The boy's first name, John, had been suggested by Julia's older sister Mimi Smith.

John's father, Alf 'Freddie' Lennon, was a merchant seaman, away at sea at the time of his only child's birth. Fred's roots lay in Ireland – Liverpool was then regarded, only half-jokingly, as being 'the capital of Ireland' – and he was later to claim that his own father was a member of Ireland's famous Kentucky Minstrels (an assertion summarily dismissed by other members of the family).

Freddie was 'forthright', a euphemism for awkwardness or for 'being bolshy'. A quality that could only make his marriage to the talented, 'flighty' Julia Stanley even more of a rollercoaster (she was a cinema usherette at the time, nightly soaking up vast silver-screen dreams that few men, least of all Freddie Lennon, could ever have made come true).

Within three years of their registry-office wedding the relationship – damaged by a war that extended Fred's absences – was effectively over. Although the overseas father would often send money to help his newborn son, he didn't actually see the child until the latter was almost six.

The Second World War, again starting in Europe, once more brought change to America's security forces. The FBI did monitor some of the activities of America's pro-Nazi German Bund, although the Bund did not suffer any serious harassment before December 1941 (as late as the autumn of 1941 Nazi propaganda movies were still being screened in American cinemas, mainly in Yorkville, then the German quarter of New York City).

But 1941 was a key year in every sense – during the 12 months between 1940 and 1942, almost everything changed. The European war went global in spectacular fashion, as Nazi Germany invaded Soviet Russia in June. Secret memos concerning the Wannsee Conference flew back and forth in Berlin in December. Hitler himself did not bother to attend the conference, which didn't actually convene until January 1942, but it was at that meeting, in a leafy Berlin suburb, that the decision was taken to implement the genocidal 'Final Solution'. 'Who, today, remembers the Ottoman massacre of the Armenians?' Hitler had casually asked, in order to show how easily he felt such a crime could be forgotten.

In July 1941 the French Vichy regime, having already ceded half of France to Nazi aggressors, then allowed their Far Eastern fascist ally, Imperial Japan, to take over Indochina.

This was the area dominated by the nation later to be known as Viet Nam, later still to be called by the one-word name Vietnam. While the Japanese forces there did not often behave with quite the same ruthlessness they exhibited in Nanking and the Philippines, the locals did still suffer, far more than their French 'protectors'. The only real opposition to the 'official invasion' came from Ho Chi Minh's native communist guerrillas.

From Indochina, Tojo's Nippon warriors could strike out at British Malaya – which, of course, they did, the very same day that America's Pearl Harbor was struck, 7 December 1941. The latter was a disaster for the US Navy, particularly its Naval Intelligence wing, which had no idea such a whirlwind was about to wreak havoc on America's doorstep. With the US and Japan involved, the conflict that had begun in Poland in 1939 had truly become a world war in 1941.

Back in Liverpool, 1941 was also an important year for little John Winston Lennon – by the year's end his mother, like his father, had also deserted him. She'd decided that it would be best if the child were raised by his Aunt Mimi and her quiet husband George in the middle-class heart of nearby Woolton.

Although Julia Lennon initially visited the child on a fairly regular basis, her appearances became less and less frequent – mainly because of two new romances, the second long-lasting, and the three children that these later produced.

In the US, the CIA's predecessor, the obliquely named Office of Strategic Studies (OSS), also came into being in 1941, on the orders of President Franklin D Roosevelt. Its founder was one Colonel William 'Big Bill' Donovan, a lawyer from the Deep South.

From the start, as its own OSS War Report stated, it was envisaged that journalists would be used in order to engage in 'psychological warfare', while it was made clear to OSS staff operatives that 'psychological warfare' was a brief wide enough to include misinformation, sabotage and even 'assassination'.

Whether a liberal Democrat president like FDR had ever genuinely wanted to work with Donovan in the long term is debatable – but the latter was acceptable to US military intelligence and Roosevelt was an ill man – he would not outlive the war. He was also already in debt to the US military after the events of 1934.

Back then, an attempted *coup d'état* by a far-right element of the US army would have succeeded – and FDR *would* have been assassinated – had not most officers at the time stayed loyal (many, no doubt, with some reluctance).

This failed coup has almost been written out of American history – some historians don't bother to mention it at all – but it *was* serious for several reasons. Firstly, because the coup itself could, just, have succeeded in changing US and world history. The attempt was also important because, even if one forgot the shoot-out and the deaths, it did still show the depth of feeling on the American Right.

Even Roosevelt's sensibly moderate reforms were to be opposed by any means possible, even violence. This was treason of the highest order, an armed attack on the president (an attack, moreover, that was supported by some of the very men who had previously pledged to defend him, their head of state). This was a lesson with deadly implications, an important lesson that few of Roosevelt's Democratic successors seem to have taken on board.

One lesson that his opponents did soon learn was that FDR's constituency – unions, blacks, Latinos, Jews, Catholics, small farmers, women and middle-class liberals – was unstoppable at the ballot box. The Republicans might have had the Rockefellers, Howard Hughes and William Randolph 'Citizen Kane' Hearst – and all the tens of millions of dollars that such men could raise – but it wasn't enough to defeat the masses.

FDR won the 1932, 1936, 1940 and 1944 elections – by which point the Right gave up trying to defeat him and concentrated on changing the law instead. Their aim was to prevent such a popular personality ever again holding sway and they eventually succeeded – an amendment was passed that prevented any future president from holding office for more than two terms...

The newly created OSS was to handle America's overseas enemies just as the FBI dealt with the domestic variety. Because these enemies would sometimes overlap – a US citizen travelling abroad to sell state secrets, say, or a German spy working within the US – so the two agencies had to liaise from point one. This cooperation was something that had been emphasised by British spymaster, Bill Cavendish-Bendinck, a former soldier who'd been irritated by the constant in-fighting amongst London's various intelligence services.

Cavendish-Bendinck was, initially, something of an influence on the fledgling OSS (after Pearl Harbor the British and Americans were allies in all theatres of the conflict; not because the US had declared war on Nazi Germany – the Bund and the right-wing of Republican Party were still strong enough to prevent Roosevelt doing this – but purely because Hitler had declared war on the US, part of the Fuhrer's vain attempt to get Imperial Japan to declare war on Russia).

Even at the height of the war, though, there were those on the right within the US intelligence services who'd have preferred an armistice to outright victory over the people they considered natural allies – the fascists of Imperial Japan and Nazi Germany.

There are certain incidents that look remarkably suspicious today, in an age when double-cross and double-think are widely known about – if not widely accepted. In mid-June 1942, just after the Battle of

Midway had seen the US Navy best the forces of Imperial Japan for the first time, the *Chicago Tribune* newspaper ran a front-page story detailing how the triumph had been made possible by the Navy's 'magic' code-breaking system. The latter, one of America's most important wartime secrets, had been put at serious risk by a story that could have cost millions of Allied lives.

Luckily, Tojo's high command did not believe the newspaper story, but it was not mere coincidence that the *Chicago Tribune* was actually owned by Robert McCormick, a one-time colonel who had friends in Washington DC (the isolationist McCormick was also violently opposed to both Roosevelt and the whole anti-fascist war effort).

During the 1944 US election, FDR's Republican opponent Thomas Dewey had planned to reveal that Roosevelt had been in possession of the Japanese and German naval codes for years – thus trying to make FDR responsible for not foreseeing the Pearl Harbor attack. Such a 'revelation' from a future president would have forced the Axis powers to change codes and coding systems – again thousands of lives could have been lost. Under massive behind-the-scenes pressure, Dewey was forced to reconsider and then finally withdraw his code-exposure plan.

In May 1945 Nazi Germany surrendered as the OSS – occasionally helped by the Vatican and British Military Intelligence – began to secretly smuggle hundreds of Nazi war criminals down the 'rat-runs', the secret routes that led to the US and South America. Although unspoken anti-Semitism no doubt played a part in these actions, the two main reasons were loot and anti-communism (several US generals had reached Western Germany with the words, 'On to Moscow!').

Martin Bormann, Hitler's deputy and the keeper of the Nazi's Swiss bank-account codes, was saved by the loot factor. Although he was supposed to have died in Berlin in May 1945, the body actually belonged to an unfortunate lookalike, for Bormann himself had been whisked off to Britain in a joint OSS/MI action (the action's code name, according to former Royal Navy spy John Ainsworth-Davis, was OPJB).

Through Bormann the Allies got most of the Nazi cash out of Switzerland but they then, bizarrely, allowed him to flee to Paraguay and a life of luxury – he died there some 14 years later, in a red soil area, which accounts for the *terra rossa* earth found around Bormann's skull after its official, miraculous 'discovery' in Berlin in 1973 (in an area that had been thoroughly searched several times at the end of the war, an area – like the rest of Berlin – that is completely bereft of red soil).

The Bormann episode, not fully revealed until 1996, is telling in several ways – it showed the immorality of the western intelligence services, which were prepared to work with, and then grant a life of ease to, a war criminal responsible for many thousands of deaths. It also demonstrated the lengths those services were prepared to go to in order cover up their activities – dozens had died in the secret operation, including the unwitting Bormann lookalike who'd already undergone imprisonment and extensive plastic surgery before his untimely death.

The evacuation of another top Nazi – Klaus Barbie, the French-based 'Butcher of Lyons' – was also conducted in 1945, Barbie being prized for his extensive knowledge of France's resistance fighters, many of whom were socialists or communists.

The Russians were not informed, of course, for the Cold War had already begun...

In Vietnam, then still French Indochina, the returning Gaullic authorities decided that maintaining law and order – that is, combating the spread of socialist Ho Chi Minh's growing popularity in the north – would best be served by a huge new infusion of armed militia. Indochinese natives were at first extremely shocked and then visibly angered when the French expedited this strategy by first freeing and then re-arming some of the Imperial Japanese troops that had oppressed the locals for over four years...

In Liverpool, John Lennon began to attend Dovedale Primary School, a stone's throw from the Strawberry Fields Children's Home with its sprawling gardens. His first year seemed happy enough – the war, and the fading threat of bombing, was finally over and he was beginning to settle down well with Aunt Mimi and her kindly spouse.

But massive ructions shook the following summer holidays. Lennon's father Fred returned to the 'pool with the idea of emigrating 'down under', to the new land of New Zealand. And he now wanted to take with him the son he hardly knew.

By then, however, mother Julia had – perhaps partly because of Fred's new interest – suddenly decided she wanted the little boy back herself.

In a cheap Blackpool hotel the tearful child watched as the increasingly vicious arguments raged back and forth amid the peeling wallpaper and cracked windows. And then, agony of agonies, the little boy was asked to choose between his previously absent father and his previously uninterested mother.

Lennon chose his father, then, minutes later, sobbing in the street, he changed his mind and tried to chase after his departing mother. A disappointed Fred did the decent thing for once and withdrew quietly. John then stayed with his mother – but only for a few days. Before the week was out Julia Lennon had returned to her new partner John Dykins, after dropping off an emotionally shattered young Master Lennon, once more back at his Aunt Mimi's…

Looking back over all this more than six decades later, the chain of personal and international events seems strangely interwoven, as inevitable as death and taxes – desertion and secrecy, lookalikes and assassinations, public morality and secret crime, West and East, hot war and Cold War. Britain, Germany, America, Japan, Vietnam…

The changes within the above nations were later to impact heavily on that small child, then living near the banks of the Mersey. It's as if John Lennon's destiny – his first musical residences, his biggest romance, his travels, his political protests, his life and death – had already been mapped out before he'd begun his first year in junior school, before he'd even spoken his first words…

3 Art For Art's Sake

'Presidents and kings come and go but the CIA goes on forever.'
— *Anonymous*

The Central Intelligence Agency (CIA) was created in 1947 – the same year as the House of Un-American Activities Committee first began its hearings, the start of the anti-red witchhunts that Senator Joe McCarthy later took to frightening heights of hysteria.

The CIA was the child of the OSS and its even more secretive OFC branch. From the start the CIA saw its role in the widest possible terms. It wasn't just the obvious targets – overseas spies and troublemakers – that were to be covered. Foreign and domestic anarchists, communists, socialists and even their alleged 'fellow travellers' – liberals and civil liberties lobbyists – were to be watched every step of the way and in every single sphere of life.

The fact that much of this intruded on FBI territory didn't worry the new organisation's directorate overly – collaboration with Hoover's boys was usually pretty good and when it came down to any kind of confrontation the CIA had the ultimate card to play. The latter was a set of photos of Hoover and Colson engaged in homosexual activity – copies of these photos were owned by the ruthless James J Angleton, ex-OSS officer and CIA counter-intelligence chief. There is, of course, a certain grim irony in this – Hoover himself gets caught out, the blackmailer blackmailed – but the end result was neither good for the US nor for democracy.

On those few occasions that Hoover tried to confront the CIA over its growing excesses, his position was weakened from the start by the blurred black-and-white photos that Angleton possessed. Later on, such a situation was to lead to several horrifying conclusions.

The CIA never seriously tried to have Hoover removed from office for the very same reason – why lose a man you can easily threaten, to have him replaced with a stranger you might have no 'dirt' on?

With the coast clear, and assured of FBI help, the CIA began to infiltrate every post-war industry – even those connected with the arts. In the post-war fine-art world, for instance, there was great concern at the way major figures like Picasso had so publicly embraced socialism (something that was arguably expressed in pre-war works like *Guernica* and post-war efforts such as *Charnel House*).

Determined that the Cold War art agenda was not going to be influenced in any way, shape or form by the left, the CIA created a series of fronts to promote artists whose work – whatever its true, long-term merit – and general attitudes were deemed apolitical. A useful distraction.

The Congress for Cultural Freedom, Britain's *Encounter* magazine and the American Newspaper Guild were merely the tip of a very large iceberg of liberal media endeavours that secretly received tens of thousands of CIA dollars (something that the US press did eventually reveal, but not until the spring of 1966 – almost 20 years after the arts and media infiltration programme had begun).

The price of paintings by abstract expressionists Jackson Pollock and Mark Rothko soared at an incredible rate during the '50s, even though the former's work was mainly drips and splashes while the latter dealt principally with mesmerisingly large blocks of blended colours.

Although part of that can be put down to inflation – and a larger part to 'art inflation' – much of the rise in interest for works considered mildly daring at the time simply cannot be accounted for – unless the CIA's efforts are taken into account.

While Pollock was mostly too busy drinking to care that much – he was dead drunk by 1955, dead by 1956 – Rothko was a man very much at odds with the brash ethos of modern America and he saw his own contemplative canvasses in a vaguely subversive light – a notion that lasted until 1959 when he was offered the commission to produce a large piece of work for an upscale restaurant in Manhattan's Wall Street district.

Here was the perfect opportunity for subversion, for cocking an artistic snook right under the very noses of the new cheque-book czars, a chance to make the undeserving rich choke on their caviar. But it was not to be. After merely ordering a single meal in the restaurant – and even before, it's said, the first course had arrived – Rothko saw the impossibility of it all. It was blatantly obvious to anyone of any intelligence – nothing in his oblique style could possibly cause comment, let alone offence, in such an atmosphere of deal making, gossip and conspicuous consumption. He wasn't going to break any boundaries in Wall Street, only provide chewing gum for the eyes, a backdrop for power brunches and discordant, drunken celebrations in the evening (a disgusted Rothko swiftly refused the commission, thus losing several thousand dollars).

Andy Warhol is another US artist who allegedly received a boost – again unwittingly – from the same tainted source. And it is true that after 1965, when he stopped silk-screening his more disturbing images of Americana – car crashes, police attacks on civil-rights marchers, Jackie Kennedy in mourning – exposure, and demand, for his work went through the roof (his block-coloured celeb pictures continue to rise in value even today, a self-fulfilling principle in art once someone, or something, has started the ball rolling).

America's pop and op artists thus became the world's most important artists – a lead they held through the '50s and much of the '60s. A first for the United States.

Thus brightly coloured consumerism was to be celebrated, not attacked, and even though some of the above works were done with irony – and sometimes even brilliance – the end result was the same; the founding of a strong new tradition that increasingly demanded that 'art' could be literally anything – from a blank canvas to a shiny cartoon to an unmade bed – as long as it was without practicality, meaning or politics (and preferably without any of the above three).

John Lennon was aware of pop art and like many of his contemporaries he had a sneaking regard for some of it. In a dreary post-war Britain of drizzle and rationing – still paying back its Lend Lease loans to a US determined to ensure the complete death of the Empire – it was perhaps inevitable. Everything was black and white in the UK of the '50s, from the two TV stations, to the newspapers, to the children's comics and even the cartoons.

There was family fun and safety, and jobs for life, as well as a glorious past, but even these were celebrated in films that were 99 per cent monochrome. Anything in full colour, let alone an exciting new art genre, would have had appeal.

Lennon began his first term at Liverpool College of Art in September 1957, some weeks before his 17th birthday. The fledgling teddy boy teenager had failed his 'O' Level exams – all nine of them – and would not have got into college at all had it not been for the quality of his art work and the enthusiasm he'd displayed at the interview.

However, the enthusiasm was short-lived. Lennon's sketches came in later and later, fewer and fewer. Painting was all right but music, that was the real thing, his real love, specifically rock 'n' roll. Bright technicolour films like the Elvis movies and *The Girl Can't Help It*, fed the fantasy of widescreen stardom (movies affecting him as they had his mother before him). Lennon even recruited his biggest art-college pal – the talented Stuart Sutcliffe – into the dream of rock 'n' roll success.

And dream it certainly seemed. By the autumn of 1957 Britain had produced only one rock 'n' roll star and he, Tommy Steele, had quickly shifted into the more lucrative ballads market, mainly to prolong his career (Steele was to release only two more uptempo numbers on single after 1957). The ascendance of the second big English rock act, Cliff Richard And His Drifters – later called The Shadows after name problems with the US originals – was over a year away, in late 1958. No British act of any musical genre had ever had an American Number One or even sold particularly well in continental Europe. Music was not a major breadwinner for an economy that had even rationed its sweets until Lennon was a teenager.

Britain exported family cars, fast but unreliable motorcycles, radios, steel, coal, the occasional film and a bankrupt sense of superiority – mainly to the former Empire: the Commonwealth of Canada, Australia, New Zealand, Hong Kong, Singapore, Nigeria, Uganda, South Africa and Malaya.

In fact the Southeast Asian state of Malaya was the site of another British export relevant to this book – 'hearts and minds'. As with most other Asian colonies, the post-war period in Malaya saw a growing resentment of government and big business managed by representatives of the European 'mother countries', the imperial states who had failed to protect their 'subjects' from the assaults of Imperial Japan.

This anger blended with support for communist guerrillas – the latter had often been the only effective opposition to Tojo's troops – which mushroomed after the war. The initial belief among many of the colonists was that life could go as it had before 1941. In the neo-racist parlance of the ex-pats, the locals 'simply weren't up to the job' of running the place and it was too early to even think about letting them try. A little patience on all sides might have bought peaceful resolutions into play but patience, post-1945, was in short supply.

When Chairman Mao's guerrillas finally completed their takeover of China in 1948, the trickle of support for neighbouring revolutions gradually became a river and then a flood. In October 1951 Malaya's British High Commissioner Sir Henry Gurney was killed in a communist ambush. Armed attacks on British forces had been rising in the area for months – along with terrorist attacks on economic targets such as rubber plantations – and Sir Henry Gurney's killing signified the real start of the 'Malayan Emergency'.

Thousands of young British conscripts were sent to deprive the red guerrillas of local support. The official response was not purely military, instead the stick was to be balanced with the carrot. It was the birth of the so-called 'hearts and minds' programme.

In the jungles and along the rivers, areas of most support to the insurgents were isolated and, in many cases, depopulated. Unlike the French in Algeria, the British rarely resorted to massacre. The natives were, instead, to have their hearts won over with free medical treatment for children, extensive literacy courses, the digging of freshwater wells etc... If they 'had' to be moved it was usually done with some kind of order and decency.

The problem was, however, that the atmosphere of oppression still remained – troops belonging to a distant European country, foreign soldiers of a foreign race, were evicting thousands of locals in a desperate attempt to defeat armed rebels who were able to slip from territory to territory overnight.

The Malayan Emergency continued through most of the '50s. By the end of the decade, the British seemed to have won – the terrorists were on the run, local and national government had kept going and the local resentment of London seemed slight. As the Malayan Federation moved towards limited independence, it looked as if the Mother Country might even manage to keep its export market for finished goods.

One observer of all this was British writer Anthony Burgess, then working within the UK Civil Service out in Malaya. The future author of *A Clockwork Orange* met several times with US intelligence officials – men fascinated by the seemingly successful 'hearts and minds' scheme. And men who had schemes of their own.

It was at this time that CIA agents first began work on MK/ULTRA, a CIA 'mind control' scheme born of the ARTICHOKE and BLUEBIRD projects. Although it was supposed to be purely to help with interrogations, the programme rapidly became one that the CIA hoped would yield either assassins – to eliminate foreign troublemakers – or 'patsies', the fall guys on whom killings could be blamed.

It was believed that, with sufficient work, neither assassin nor 'patsy' would have any idea of what crimes they'd committed or why (the subject of Anthony Burgess' 1962 book *A Clockwork Orange* was aversion therapy, the manipulation of the brain – years later author Roger Lewis tried to access the CIA's Anthony Burgess file; he was told that, whether such a file existed or not, it was not available for viewing for reasons of 'national security').

The CIA does not have a gloriously honourable record when it comes to mind control. After starting the MKULTRA plan, allegedly at Fort Bliss, the Agency soon shifted its operations into several different US cities and using several different techniques – manipulation of the brain's alpha waves, sodium pentathol, the so-called 'truth drug', deep hypnosis, auto suggestion and hallucinogenic drugs.

Huge doses of lysergic acid, LSD, were dished out. These hallucinogenic drugs were not given to volunteers, who might have been prepared or at least willing, but to unwitting CIA workers and 'outside Agency' civilians. Sometimes these doses were given to casual passers-by, lured into hotel rooms by false invitations or by hired prostitutes. At other times they were injected – often with big doses of mescaline – into those attending hospitals for minor psychiatric ailments.

In 1953 alone at least two American civilians – Frank Olson and Harold Blauer – died in these experiments. The former was a scientist working for the CIA who crashed through a ninth-floor hotel window and then jumped to his death. The latter, Blauer, was a depressed tennis pro, who died foaming at the mouth after his hospital deliberately gave him a massive mescaline shot on CIA orders. The dead men's families were not, of course, told the real reason for the death of their husbands and fathers.

The CIA was busy on other fronts too during the mid '50s. The democratically elected but left-wing Arbenz government of Guatemala was overthrown in 1954 in a bloody CIA-backed *coup d'état*. It was a coup that was to leave the small Central American state in the hands of generals for the next 40 years – during which time they and their death squads killed 100,000 Indians as well as thousands of opposition activists. Nearly all of these victims were unarmed civilians and among their number were tens of thousands of senior citizens and young children.

The same year saw the first major inter-power conference on Indochina. There the French colonial forces had been fought to a standstill, despite heavy Agency backing, by the guerrillas supporting Ho Chi Minh's leftist Viet Ninh regime in Hanoi in the north.

At 1954's Geneva Conference, America's representative, John Foster Dulles, had been spoiling for a fight, for a chance to extend the first Vietnamese war. But skilful manoeuvring by Britain's foreign secretary Anthony Eden and China's Zhou Enlai led instead to a French agreement to withdraw. The treaty also gave Cambodia and Laos the chance to establish themselves as independent nations, while the Buddhist socialist North Vietnam and the Catholic capitalist South Vietnam were to remain separate countries temporarily, until nationwide elections could be held.

But the CIA's own secret polls quickly revealed the inevitability of Ho Chi Minh's electoral victory at the ballot box and the US president of the time, Eisenhower, was later to privately admit that some 80 per cent of the Indochinese would inevitably have voted for Minh – if given the chance. But they weren't allowed that option, as the US moved heaven and earth to make sure the nationwide elections were postponed indefinitely. In Guatemala, as in Vietnam, when democracy offered the wrong result – that is, a left-of-centre government – or even just the possibility of the wrong result, it was to be ignored. After all, the right excuses had been offered and debated, of course. It was a position of discreet hypocrisy that was obtained throughout most of the 20th century. These machinations were – are – public knowledge in much of the Third World, but not in Middle America where many citizens still do not understand the southern hemisphere's bitter resentment of the superpower that so often armed and supported their dictatorial oppressors.

The US answer in divided Viet Nam was eventually to cancel the elections while donating arms and guns to the South. This did not end the tensions in the police state south of the 20th parallel which, while ruled by a wealthy Catholic minority, was in essence also a Buddhist country with a Buddhist majority.

In 1960, communist guerrillas known as the Vietcong started the National Liberation Front (NLF). From the start the NLF was clever enough to court the favour of the southern peasantry; unpopular priests were beaten, brutal landlords were shot, their gunmen driven out and the food surpluses of the bigger farms stolen and redistributed. All the US-backed South Vietnamese authorities could offer to counter this was the threat of torture and/or summary execution to anyone who was caught helping the Vietcong. Such a response was crude but it was not, in the end, effective.

4 Love Me Do

'I just wanted them to be my friends, that's why I managed
The Who, that's why I managed any group.'
– *Pete Meadon*

Brian Epstein had been looking for The Beatles for years. Not that he
knew their name – or even that they'd turn out to be a rock 'n' roll group
– but he was looking for something. Anyone who was cultured or Jewish
or wealthy could often feel a little out of place in Liverpool then. Epstein
was all three.

He was also gay in an age when such a lifestyle was completely illegal
– at best it meant constant vigilance and trusting the 'kindness of strangers',
at worst it meant a lifetime of blackmail, harassment, public shame and
short, sharp prison sentences. The sensitivity that gave him certain insights
also left Epstein with a hefty dose of guilt over his sexual preferences.

Serving record-store customers, even when most had a certain respect
for him, was not really his idea of fun. But the family music shop was
the one place where he saw, and could talk to, young people. Those in
their teens or early 20s, those who were a few years – and several lifetimes
– younger than him, those who seemed so much freer and happier than
he ever did.

And then, in November 1961, the *something* casually walked into
the NEMS music emporium. That something was a teenage boy asking
for a German record by Tony Sheridan and The Beatles (the German
label actually called them The Beat Brothers). Epstein thought he had
heard of the band but couldn't think where, since the store didn't normally
stock German imports (he, or one his acquaintances, may have seen the
name in Bill Harry's *Merseybeat* magazine, which had been launched

that summer, complete with Lennon's humorous history of The Beatles). And then the boy told him that the band weren't actually Germans, they were locals, an underground 'beat combo' who were playing regularly at the Cavern Club.

On 9 November 1961, Brian Epstein determined to check out this new 'Merseybeat' group. John Lennon and Paul McCartney had then just returned from a brief holiday in Paris with Jurgen Vollmer, one of their Hamburg art friends. Vollmer had persuaded them to replace their teddy-boy quiffs with the 'French-style' long scruffy fringe that was later to be called the 'moptop'.

In the basement heat of the Cavern, with their wild hair and black leather, The Beatles – both toughened and seasoned by their endless Hamburg nights – seemed irresistible to Epstein. He loved their semi-educated roughness, the fact that they were handsome, spontaneous, talented and dangerous. And free. Everything he'd wanted to be at their age, everything he wanted to be *now*. Whether they could ever be polished enough to reach the very top was another thing entirely. But to Epstein that no longer mattered, he was already hooked.

He instantly saw that Lennon was the leader and spent most of the next few days winning him over. Within a month he'd become The Beatles' first serious manager, promising to use his position as one of Liverpool's leading record retailers to arrange auditions with major labels.

On 9 December they played their first live event in the south of England. Only 18 punters turned up to see them in Aldershot's Princess Hall. If their faith in Epstein's organisational abilities was shaken they were rapidly proved wrong after he pulled a few strings and arranged a New Year's Day audition at Decca Records – one of the biggest labels in the UK and the home of Tommy Steele, The Tornados and Cliff Richard.

The Beatles attended the Decca audition in a different musical world to the one Lennon had fallen in love with some five years before. Rock 'n' roll had been eclipsed by pop, by a string of smooth young crooners. Some, like Ricky Nelson, actually had talent, but most were practically interchangeable: Fabian, Bobby Vee and many more – just like their British equivalents. Glossy, pretty and manufactured. The boy bands of their day.

Of the original rockers, Elvis had never fully recovered his musical drive after being drafted into the US Army, Chuck Berry had been jailed for violating the Mann Act, Buddy Holly and Eddie Cochran died in travelling accidents while Gene Vincent fled to Britain and then France after union problems. In Britain, Johnny Kidd had broken through some two years before with seminal rockers 'Shakin' All Over' and 'Please Don't Touch'. But he was the only one, the exception that proved the rule. Even Cliff Richard, who'd sparked riots at one point, now sounded like one of the new pop dream boys.

The Beatles already had quite a few Lennon-McCartney songs but Epstein had wanted The Beatles to play mostly covers at the audition. And, on New Year's Day 1962, that's exactly what they did at Decca's studios in West Hampstead, London. Lennon, Harrison and McCartney resplendent with their longer, ungreased hair and drummer Pete Best still with his trademark quiff (Stuart Sutcliffe had effectively left the group by then, as he'd stayed behind in Hamburg to paint with his German girlfriend, Astrid Kircherr).

The Beatles' rock and pop covers, balanced with some McCartney-dominated ballads, did not go down well. Decca's chief A&R Dick Rowe rejected the band with the words that have now become almost legendary, 'guitar bands are on the way out' (though, for some reason, that didn't stop him signing Dagenham's Brian Poole And The Tremeloes the same day).

The Beatles' disappointment was alleviated, at least a little, by their first radio session for BBC Manchester in March. 'Dream Baby', 'Memphis Tennessee' (sung by Lennon) and the early Motowner 'Please Mister Postman' were recorded and duly broadcast the next day. The radio plays clinched it for Epstein – during the last week of March the band finally agreed to his suggestion that they wear suits on stage.

Lennon saw the matching suits as the first and, in some ways, the biggest, compromise of the Beatle years. It sounds an excessive, almost fashion-victim comment but it's hard to exaggerate the importance of clothes to young people in Britain from the mid '40s to the late '80s.

Clothes could get you – or lose you – a good job, a steady girlfriend, police attention or a new set of friends. Clothes were an indication of class, attitude, imagination and even politics. The Beatles' suits were chic, collarless and as black as the leather they'd just dumped...but they were still *suits*, the uniform of every bank clerk and junior civil servant. Suits, even sharp ones, just didn't cut it as far as young musicians were concerned. But, in order to make it to, in Lennon's words, 'the toppermost of the poppermost' you had to do what was necessary, you had to be a tough bastard. And the Fab Four, he once boasted, were the biggest bastards going.

In April the band returned to Hamburg, to a Star Club residency and the news that young Stuart Sutcliffe was dead – killed by a brain haemorrhage (probably the result of a beating dished out by thugs after a gig in Liverpool, which didn't stop various writers, as well as members of the Sutcliffe family, from later claiming that it was Lennon's violence that was responsible for his best friend's death).

Lennon reacted exactly the same way he had when his mother and stepfather had died – after laughing hysterically for a few moments he faked indifference (though it was also a kind of tough love, forcing Sutcliffe's girlfriend Astrid to live, to go out and go on – she later said he helped save her from endless depression).

A few weeks later Epstein sent a telegram from England with good news – EMI had agreed to audition the band. EMI was then the biggest label outside of America – and its US subsidiary Capitol even managed to sell millions Stateside with big-name artists such as Frank Sinatra.

Epstein didn't tell them that the EMI producer-A&R in question, George Martin, worked for Parlophone, one of the smaller EMI labels. It was also a label more usually associated with novelty or comedy records by the likes of Peter Sellers, Bernard Cribbins or Charlie Drake. By now, though, Epstein was hip enough not to say anything that would cut into his boys' confidence – though he did add 'PLEASE REHEARSE NEW MATERIAL' to the foot of the telegram.

Paul's ballads and the usual rock standards hadn't worked at the Decca audition and the band were fast running out of time – Bill Harry had started the *Merseybeat* magazine for good reason, namely because there were already dozens of beat groups playing live in Liverpool (by the end of 1962 there were over 90). Many already had hundreds of fans

– bands such as Kingsize Taylor And The Dominoes, The Big Three, Rory Storm And The Hurricanes and Gerry And The Pacemakers. At any time any one of them could be signed up to steal The Beatles' thunder and then claim the Mersey sound as their very own, thus relegating the rest of the others to being, at best, also-rans. The Parlophone audition had to be The Beatles' best – they might not get another.

At EMI's Abbey Road Studios on 6 June 1962 the band were told to play four numbers. They did a Coasters' cover plus 'Love Me Do' and two other originals. McCartney handled most of the lead vocals, with John singing 'Ask Me Why'. Despite having reservations about Pete Best's drumming, George Martin expressed serious interest in the band. The actual decision to sign the band was taken a few days later – after, allegedly, Epstein had phoned EMI and told them in no uncertain terms that his NEMS shops would no longer stock EMI products if the band were rejected.

With EMI's permission Martin signed the band and within days the major label's influence began to get results. On 11 June the BBC Light Programme – then Britain's only national radio station – did its first session with The Beatles for the Beeb's *Here We Go* show.

July 1962 saw the very first Lennon lyric to appear on record as Darren Young aka Johnny Gentle had his 'I've Just Fallen For Someone' issued as a single, complete with an uncredited middle eight by The Beatles' founder. The next month things were anything but gentle as Pete Best was finally fired. The drummer had been with them for years but Martin's critical comments had added to a growing rift between Best and the rest of The Beatles (principally, it's said, over Best's refusal to lose his somewhat dated teddy-boy quiff – if this is true it must make it the most expensive haircut in question since it eventually cost him over £200 million…).

After Best left – to be replaced with the Hurricanes' Ringo Starr, an old pal from Hamburg – some of his more dedicated Cavern Club fans physically attacked both Ringo and Harrison, with Lennon saving the latter from a severe beating.

August was a hectic month at the Cavern for John Lennon, even aside from the Harrison fight. Before one gig his bottle-blonde girlfriend, the beautiful Cynthia Powell, privately told him that she was pregnant. They were married within days and on 22 August Granada TV sent a film crew to cover the Cavern Club and its strange array of beat bands. The Beatles were filmed topping the bill as they performed 'Kansas City' and the uptempo jealous-guy anthem 'Some Other Guy'.

On 1 October 1962, with their first 45 just four days away, The Beatles finally signed an official management contract with Brian Epstein's NEMS Enterprises Limited. It seems a curiously dated document now. James McCartney and Harold Harrison signed for their sons, as the boys were under 21, while NEMS management solemnly promised to do its best to promote 'a group of musicians to be known as The Beatles...in the following branches of the entertainment industry:- (a) Vaudeville and revue (b) Motion pictures (c) Balls and dances, whether of a public or private nature (d) radio and television broadcasting (e) Concerts, private parties, cabarets (f) Phonographic and tape recording (g) Sponsorship projects...'.

The contract was to run for five years. But under Clause One's proviso, either party could terminate with just three months' notice, as long as that notice was delivered 'by registered post' – Epstein, despite the EMI deal, was giving himself an out (on 22 January 1963, though, with 'Love Me Do' a hit and 'Please Please Me' picking up plenty of airplay, Epstein persuaded the band to cancel his op-out proviso).

In purely monetary terms it was not the 'Mister Ten Per Cent' contract of showbiz legend. Epstein was to get 15 per cent of The Beatles' earnings if those earnings should total less than £400 per week. This management cut rose to 20 per cent if the group's received monies exceeded £400 per week but were less than £800. If the group's earnings broke the £800 per week mark (perhaps £18,000 in current values) then NEMS/Epstein were to get a whacking 25 per cent.

From late 1963 onwards Epstein was thus to be the best-paid Beatle of all. (Sadly, the inexperienced NEMS MD wasn't so good at extracting percentages from EMI. From the start Epstein was said to have been convinced that EMI boss Sir Joseph Lockwood, as an English gentleman, couldn't possibly sanction a deal that was unfair to any artist. With a good recording royalty then being between eight and ten per cent, Epstein accepted a deal that, in real terms, got the group a lot less than five –

much later it was renegotiated upwards to prevent embarrassment for either Epstein or EMI.)

Two weeks after signing with NEMS, The Beatles appeared live on Granada TV to promote their original 'Love Me Do' debut. Although their fan base had leapt from hundreds to thousands over night, the national press had still not noticed the screaming girls who mobbed the band whenever they were north of Watford – perhaps partly because the US-Soviet confrontation known as the Cuba Crisis had selfishly grabbed the headlines by taking the globe to the brink of World War Three.

After three days of the Cuba Crisis people starting cracking sick jokes in the morning, 'Well, we're still here then!' After five days people stopped laughing. Across the world billions held their breath as millions frantically prayed. American and NATO forces were, like those of the Warsaw Pact, placed on red alert as fleets of jets and bombers stood ready on the ground while others circled in the air – champing at the bit for the Go-Code, the last order…

In a crumbling garret, Robert 'Bob Dylan' Zimmerman began to furiously scribble the song 'A Hard Rain's A-Gonna Fall'. It was made up of single lines from all the various unfinished songs he no longer believed he'd live long enough to complete…

5 1963

'Will the people in the cheaper seats clap your hands?
And the rest of you, just rattle your jewellery.'

– John Lennon

Like 1941 before it and 1968 after, 1963 was a key year in many, many ways. Artistically, in the film world several people attempted to push the medium to a higher level. Rough cuts of the first three hours of the costume extravaganza *Cleopatra*, in today's money a $200 million movie, are said to be amongst the most dramatic ever shot. But rather than indulge director Joseph L Mankiewicz for a few weeks longer, the studio seized the footage that had already been shot and cobbled together the 'finished' article. Even then, half-finished on some levels, the Elizabeth Taylor and Richard Burton epic still garnered four Oscars.

Hollywood did, of course, make a contribution to the Cold War debate – how could it not when the 13 days of the Cuba Crisis had taken the world to the brink of oblivion? Tinseltown gave us films such as *On The Beach*, which showed the aftermath of a limited nuclear war – the planet's remaining humans gather in Australia and wait for the terminal clouds of radiocactive poison to reach them. In the final reel, as suicide pills are handed out, Salvation Army banners tell us 'There Is Still Time'.

Stanley Kubrick's chilling black comedy *Dr Strangelove (Or How I Learned To Stop Worrying And Love The Bomb)* had another take on the subject, foreseeing a nuclear disaster deliberately being provoked by a USAF officer. It wasn't issued until 1964 and its portrayal of the US military led to anguished articles in American newspapers and magazines. Another film completed in 1963 but not released until the following year was *Seven Days In May*, the story of a conspiracy by US generals to bring down a liberal Democrat president after the latter begins negotiations with the Russians to rid the world of thermonuclear weapons (after seeing a sneak preview of *Seven Days In May* President Kennedy told the director, 'that [a US Army coup] is what would happen to me if I ever tried such a deal').

Meanwhile, in England in May 1963, Joseph Losey, a Hollywood director who'd fled the McCarthy witchhunts, finally got to see his film *The Damned* hit British screens. It was his version of HI Lawrence's cult sci-fi novel *The Children Of Light* and it had been shot and edited by him way back in 1961. Among the film's rising stars were Shirley Ann Field, Viveca Lindfors and a young Oliver Reed. But Hammer Films, the producer, was used to more mainstream 'horror' and it was, quite simply, outraged by the movie's anti-nukes sensibility. After viewing it again, the company agreed to postpone its release until late 1962.

By turns, touching, thought-provoking and sinister, *The Damned* concerns liberal 'nice guy' Simon, an American tourist played by the middle-aged MacDonald Carey, who picks up a girl and eventually helps her get away from her restrictive brother King and his gang of leather-clad bike thugs (who mug Simon while singing along with the film's 'Black Leather' theme song).

The movie ends in spectacular fashion – the lovers and King stumble on a secret under-cliff 'prison' of radioactive children who've never seen daylight. The unlikely trio free the young inmates and are then hunted down before King is killed. The two lovers escape by boat, shadowed by an Army helicopter and unaware that they're already dying of radiation sickness. The children themselves are rounded up and swiftly re-imprisoned, ready once again to reluctantly serve the post-nuclear war state 'when the time comes...' (time, or lack of it, was a constant theme then).

The Damned ends with the sound of the children, now finally aware of the outside beauty they're missing, crying hopelessly – 'Help Us! Please Somebody Help Us!' – as the camera pans over the distant holidaymakers on Weymouth's glitzy beach. The cries are obviously meant to be our cries, our screams for help in a world gone MAD (Mutually Assured Destruction, the deterrent theory of nuclear weaponry).

They are also the cries of anyone – or everyone – with a damaged childhood, the 'Rosebud symbol' of the atomic age. The 'Rosebud symbol' comes from Orson Welles' pioneering 1941 film *Citizen Kane*, with its reporter's quest for the meaning of a media tycoon's dying words – to a harrowing blaze of strings we finally discover, though the reporter does not, that 'Rosebud' refers to Kane's snow sledge and the aborted childhood it represents – Lennon's own childhood was similarly deconstructed, though he turned his driving ambition into something more worthy than Kane's megalomania (some of the West's finest love songs were to burst from his cynical, long-fractured heart...).

Then the October 1962 horror of the Cuba Crisis made Hammer postpone the *The Damned*'s release for another seven months. Finally, the following May – after sneak previews of Losey's follow-up *The Servant* had already started Oscar rumours – *The Damned* was publicly screened in London – but only after some 13 minutes had been hacked out of it. Its US release, as *These After The Damned*, was postponed for another two years and even then it was only allowed out after being buried as part of a low-budget double bill.

Despite such treatment, the UK's leading indie film critic of the time, Raymond Durgnant, predicted that *The Damned* might yet be seen as 'one of the most important films of the '60s, while its screening at the first Trieste Science Fiction Film Festival led to a standing ovation before it won the festival's main award.

Although often poetic, exciting and passionate, all of the above films are visions of the crackling present, their subliminal soundtracks the buzzing rattle of the Geiger counter, and all of them – despite their brilliance – are ultimately horror films, nightmares of the non-future...

On the British music scene, in early 1963 maverick producer Joe Meek was expecting six-figure royalties from his, and Britain's, first ever American Number One hit – the strange, space-age instrumental 'Telstar' by The Tornadoes. Unfortunately the money never arrived for one of the world's very first independent producers. Instead Meek – who also designed and built his own EQs and sound compressors – was slapped with a costly writ that froze his monies for more than four years. By the time the case was settled – in Meek's favour – the gay wildman of British pop production was dead (the deep-in-debt sound wizard had blown off his own head with a shotgun a few minutes after he'd killed the landlady of his tiny Holloway Road recording studio). There was a lesson here too, of sorts. You could be as independent as you liked, but when it came to big deals and big money, then it was still the big lawyers and the big distributors – like the big studios – who always called the shots. The Beatles would change that, at least for a time, but it was a change that came too late for Joe Meek and many others.

John, Paul, George and Ringo had started 1963 with their only single hit to date – 'Love Me Do', top position Number 17, just for a week – dropping slowly out of the charts, despite their furious efforts to promote it during a five-date mini-tour of Scotland.

The Scottish gigs had earned them just under £200 – by the end of the year they were getting over £4,000 for the same number of concerts (over £90,000 today). The excellent rocker 'Please Please Me', was their first Number One, though the chart used by the BBC judged it to be no higher than Number Two. It was an all-out piece of pumping, melodic magic that was later refused US airplay (the Stateside radio producers were convinced it was about oral sex, which might possibly have been the case on one level but it was certainly not an explicit song in any sense and no one in British radio had considered such a possibility).

John Lennon had first played it to George Martin at their second ever session together but back then it had been a slower, Roy Orbison-type slice of melodrama. Now it had become Britain's first real rock 'n' roll hit for years.

The group themselves had also racked up three other Number One hits by year's end – the first was 'From Me To You', which charted while 'Please Please Me' was still on the hit parade. As if to add to the celebrations that April, John's young wife Cynthia gave birth to Julian Lennon – full name John Charles Julian Lennon – at Liverpool's Sefton General Hospital.

But, like his father before him, John Lennon was absent for the birth – rehearsing with the rest of the Fab Four in London. Lennon's fame, and Epstein's outdated showbiz need to keep the marriage to Cynthia secret in case it damaged record sales, meant it was another 48 hours before John was finally smuggled in to see his newborn son. Even then he had to depart early – for a one-hour Beatles gig at Birkenhead's Majestic Ballroom...

The third chart topper that year was 'She Loves You', a third-person narrative that raced out of the traps and contained the 'yeah, yeah, yeah' chorus that was to enter the language, and newspaper headlines, of the world. The last Number One of the year was 'I Want To Hold Your Hand' with its abrupt, build-up of an intro and its superb cut-dead ending. All these hits were classics and all of them were pure Beatles, though, unlike later songs, these are so much *of* the band that they have rarely been covered despite their continuing popularity. The first and last of these – 'Please Please Me' and 'I Want To Hold Your Hand' – were principally John Lennon songs.

By the time the latter was released, over half a million orders for it had been received and the word 'Beatlemania' had entered the language as the south of England and the rest of the country finally surrendered to the Fab Four. Now mobs of young teens, mainly girls, pursued them on almost every street corner and every grand entrance required decoys, fast cars and hundreds of police officers.

At November's Royal Command Performance at the Prince of Wales Theatre The Beatles, though way down the bill, stole the show. McCartney's yearning rendition of 'Till There Was You' showing the oldies that the boys could manage a decent song properly, while Lennon's knock-out attack on 'Twist And Shout' brought the house down. For the last number Lennon gave the following introduction to the assembled lords, ladies and gentlemen:

'For this number, we'd like to ask your help. Will the people in the cheaper seats clap your hands? And the rest of you, just rattle your jewellery.'

It was the perfect remark for the occasion, cheeky enough to appeal to the young and the 'young at heart' without being really offensive. Offence had already been taken though – several days before the Royal show the conservative *Daily Telegraph* newspaper had already compared The Beatles with Hitler, and their gigs with Nuremberg rallies that filled young people's heads with 'hysteria'.

Lennon himself, as with the other Beatles, had seen the growing tumult at every concert as being, in part, a sociological phenomenon. The band were just being used as an 'excuse for people to go wild'. It was fun, at first, but the constant screaming soon began to annoy them – Lennon often ended songs with a bellowed obscenity that no one could hear amid the mayhem.

He'd originally been going to use a four-letter word during the Royal Variety Show as well, which would have been British TV's very first example of heavy swearing. But he allowed a nervous Epstein to talk him out of it. It was almost certainly for the best; the outrage that followed the Sex Pistols' TV swear-in 13 years later effectively ended their live career and the subsequent pressure probably helped break up the original line-up too, since tunesmith Glen Matlock was swiftly fired – allegedly for being a Beatles' fan, according to Pistols manager Malcolm McLaren – to be replaced by the late and deeply unmusical Sid Vicious. Such fuss might just have done similar damage to The Beatles (comparisons with the Pistols are not out of place here – not, at least, in media terms – as they also caused a great outcry, making the front pages time after time, like the Fab Four and, just like The Beatles, the new John, Paul, Steve and Glen had started out playing wild gigs in strip clubs, bars and dank jazz basements).

Lennon's verbal restraint was rewarded with a dozen rave reviews in the papers – The Beatles were wits as well as musicians and composers – and they were lauded as real talents who didn't need 'off-colour' jokes or obscenities. If only the hacks had known about Lennon's planned remark...or his notoriously sick sense of humour – most of his school, college and Merseybeat jokes had mocked rabbis or the physically handicapped – perhaps something that was initially to be expected from a sarcastic 'abandoned' child of above-average intelligence (though it has to be said that the likes of Jim Morrison were far more offensive, The Doors' frontman openly laughing in the faces of those who were wheelchair-bound).

As well as handling the media, Lennon was also learning a little about recording-studio technique along the way and, like Hendrix after him, he's supposed to have even attended some mastering sessions – mastering being, in essence, the final 'mix' as a silver cutting disc is prepared, from which the moulds for thousands of vinyl copies are pressed.

At these sessions frequencies could be boosted or reduced, special effects pulled down or pushed up and vocals stressed or half-buried and compression added to give the recording some mid-level punch, usually necessary to cut through the chewing gum, rusty jukebox, half-tuned radio fog of the intended target audience. Later, John was to complain about the crude stereo mixes – 'I dunno what they were thinking of!' – that had most vocals on one side, most instruments on the other. These were used on the rare stereo releases – most radios, record decks, jukeboxes and radios were then mono, the format for which the biggest pressings were reserved and on which Lennon had worked hardest. The stereo versions were minor sellers during 1962–64 – which now makes many of them highly collectible – but it was those stereo tapes that got used on most post-'60s re-releases and compilations.

Two Beatles albums had reached Number One in the UK during 1963 – *Please Please Me* and *With The Beatles* – sets that were to spend a staggering total of two and a half years on the British album charts (they both also contained 14 tracks on each and this in an age when 11 or 12 was the norm – an act of generosity to the fans that had only happened because Lennon had insisted on it).

A Parisian residency had been booked for 1964 and tentative plans were made for some kind of American tour, after assurances from EMI's US subsidiary Capitol that the 'I Want To Hold Your Hand' single and *Meet The Beatles* album – the US version of *With The Beatles* – would finally receive serious promotion (Capitol had actually turned down the first few Beatles singles, which had then only appeared in the US on smaller labels such as Vee Jay and Swan – and it had taken the latter five months, and The Beatles' US television debut, to get 'She Loves You' into the charts).

Gerry And The Pacemakers, the young Rolling Stones and Billy J Kramer and The Dakotas all scored hits in 1963 with Lennon-McCartney songs, and in December the London *Times* and London *Sunday Times* called Lennon and McCartney the most 'outstanding' English composers of the year, the finest young talents since Beethoven's heyday

But, in the world outside England, there were several other incidents in 1963 that were to have great importance both for John Lennon and the world.

On 16 September, as Lennon travelled to Paris with wife Cynthia for a well-earned holiday, British Malaya became Malaysia – local celebrations on gaining independence rapidly escalated into attacks on the symbols of former British rule. The violence culminated in an angry mob of over 100,000 rioters sacking and burning down the British Embassy. Despite all the rhetoric and gestures – both real and fictional – the British were to lose most of their influence in Malaya. Their exports to the Asian state were to fall dramatically too.

No one in British military intelligence really wanted to talk about it – and nor did the American spooks, of course, as they were already busy applying some of the same failed philosophies in Vietnam – but the fact was now obvious to anyone with the eyes to see it; for all its short-term successes, over the long haul the 'hearts and minds' programme had simply not worked...

In October, America's liberal Democrat President Kennedy issued National Security Action memo NSAM 263 on Vietnam which, after a three-line intro, opened with the lines:

'The President approved the military recommendations contained in Section I B (1-3) of the report but directed that no formal announcement be made of the implementation of plans to withdraw 1,000 US military personnel by the end of 1963.'

Although the wording might seen ambiguous it does indicate – especially when taken together with memo NSAM 111 – that JFK was about to start pulling out of the Vietnam morass. Kennedy's own remarks to the press in September, about the war ultimately being the responsibility of the Vietnamese people, echo this theme. NSAM 263's talk of avoiding a 'formal announcement' is also understandable. Both the CIA and military chiefs of staff – like perhaps one-third of US voters – wanted American involvement in Vietnam to continue and even to escalate. There had, after all, been remarkably few US casualties up to that point.

So Kennedy was acting in defiance of all of these. As president it was his democratic right to do so, of course, but it was a right that was rarely exercised. Especially by a young, 40-something liberal Democrat president. The Vietnam withdrawal was to be low-key but real.

Presidential NSA memo NSAM 273 then reversed all this. While the rest of the ten-point document is much the same – although the line 'plausibility of denial' has been added to point seven concerning attacks on North Vietnam – the key opening paragraph about withdrawal is missing in its entirety. The withdrawal policy had effectively been put into reverse.

The reason for this reversal was quite simple. The latter, later memo is dated 26 November and was issued by a new president, a man from the Deep South, 'LBJ', one Lyndon Baines Johnson. A man convinced that the 'hearts and minds' programme, backed with sufficient military force, would soon lead to a spectacular US victory in Southeast Asia.

The reason he was president was also simple – four days before, on 22 November 1963, John F Kennedy, the 35th President of the United States of America, had been assassinated, shot to death in broad daylight in Dallas, Texas.

6 Happiness Is A Warm Gun

'So what if he [Kennedy] screwed a few women?
Every president since has screwed the entire world'
– Shirley MacLaine

Kennedy had come to power after defeating Republican Vice-President Nixon in the 1960 election, thus ending eight long years of Republican power. The latter had been the favourite to win, having been a high-profile supporter of the McCarthy witchhunts, as well as being VP between 1952 and January 1961 when JFK was inaugurated.

Having been bounced by the CIA into approving the Bay of Pigs attack on Castro's Cuba – an invasion carried out by 1,300 Cuban exiles and US mercenaries on 17 April – JFK was horrified when the locals failed to rise up in support of the incursion.

Despite coming under considerable pressure from the CIA and the US military, JFK then refused to order a massive US air strike – such a move, with the attendant deaths of thousands of civilians, was the only action that could possibly have made the invasion a 'success'.

As well as angering the USA's intelligence community and military top brass, JFK's refusal to blitz Havana also annoyed the American Mafia. The organised crime syndicates had run most of the bars, brothels and casinos in pre-Castro Cuba and military action seemed the only way they'd regain their tax-free cash cows.

In the aftermath of the Bay of Pigs fiasco, Kennedy swore he'd smash the CIA and scatter them 'into a thousand pieces.' Within weeks CIA boss Allen W Dulles was dismissed. JFK caused further outrage amongst US security forces during the October 1962 Cuba Crisis – when the Cuban installation of Soviet nuclear missiles, presumably to deter another

Bay of Pigs attack – and also to balance the missiles that had recently arrived in US bases in Turkey – led to to a US Naval blockade and a 'Mexican stand-off'.

For almost two weeks it seemed the US and Soviet Union would go to (nuclear) war, possibly ending all human life on planet earth. Bobby 'RFK' Kennedy, the Attorney General, who was JFK's brother, eventually persuaded Russian leader Khrushchev to remove the missiles, partly in exchange for a discreet US pullback in Turkey – though not before US General Curtis E LeMay had tried to spark the apocalypse by firing a missile at the Soviet Union (Curtis E LeMay was the same man whose pilots had bombed, and firebombed, Tokyo in the spring of 1945, killing over 105,000 civilians and terrifying a young Yoko Ono).

LeMay's missile, with a dud warhead, flew over a thousand miles towards the Russians – tracked all the way by frantic Red Army radar operators – before it ditched harmlessly in the sea. At the same time CIA big-wig Bill Harvey was also trying to provoke a US-Soviet war by continuing to send anti-Castro commando teams on raids along the Cuban coast – RFK discovered this and in a justifiable fury demanded that Bill Harvey be sacked (although he was temporarily removed from his post, the CIA did not, in the end, sack Bill Harvey – after all, why make a big thing over someone merely trying to start World War Three? – but instead sent him to Europe).

If this all seems extreme to the point of madness well, yes, in many ways it was, but it has to be remembered than the US at the time of the Cuba Crisis had over 500 nuclear warheads that could reach the Soviet Union and fellow Warsaw Pact countries. The Soviets had barely 20 such weapons that could hit the US mainland, plus a few more with which to hammer Britain, western Europe and Japan.

If the Soviets could be pushed into a nuclear war they would, effectively, be wiped out by America's superior atomic firepower. Of course, the Americans' European and Asian allies would suffer vast losses too and even the continental US would have said goodbye to anything from a few hundred thousand up to ten million civilians, as well as undergoing a huge climate change (no one had ever tried exploding huge 530 nuclear weapons on the same day before...).

But to the extremists, such as LeMay and many of the CIA boys, it was a price well worth paying in order to rid the planet of the scourge of 'godless communism'. Besides, if the military caught the Russians on the hop there was a chance that US losses would be slight. Possibly.

Bombing raids ordered by LeMay had already killed over 150,000 civilians during 1945 alone – calculating such losses wasn't a big novelty for him (the insane character Colonel Jack D Ripper in *Dr Strangelove* was said to have been based on Curtis E LeMay).

Thanks to RFK's efforts, though, the Cuba Crisis failed to produce World War Three – third and last in the series – but it was a close thing.

Even JFK's saner chiefs of staff had pressed him to launch air, sea and land attacks on Cuba – we now know that the Soviet missile operators on Cuba were under strict instruction to launch their deadly missiles if there was a serious US attack deep inland.

At the time, though, the US Right was convinced that the nation had suffered yet another Kennedy setback – Cuba was still 'Red' at the end of the Crisis, wasn't it? – and JFK's next moves only seemed to confirm their worst fears. In order to reduce tension and lessen the danger of another deadly misunderstanding, Kennedy and Khrushchev agreed to establish a phone 'hotline' between the White House and Moscow's Kremlin. By the time it was operational, at the end of August 1963, the US had also signed – along with Britain and the USSR – the nuclear Test Ban Treaty, an agreement that would eventually stop all open-air explosions (except those that the French still occasionally launch). To the US top brass the Test Ban Treaty was, in effect, slowing down a nuclear arms race that they felt they could win.

Insult was added to injury when Kennedy declared that the Vietnam War was 'South Vietnam's to win' and began to draw up plans to with-draw US troops. His VP, Lyndon B Johnson, disagreed with this but then, as JFK had told his secretary the same month, Johnson was not actually going to be Kennedy's running mate in the next, 1964, election.

With his moves to repeal the 27.5 per cent oil-depletion tax loophole, JFK had dared to upset the big oil companies too, particularly those run by Dallas oil billionaire HL Hunt – a Rightist fanatic who had his own intelligence network; he'd also spent millions of dollars in the '50s backing

Congressman Lyndon B Johnson, VP Richard Nixon, fellow Republican Gerald Ford as well as Senator Joe McCarthy.

Before leaving office, the Republican President Eisenhower had spoken of his worries concerning the growing power of 'the military-industrial complex'. Now, a thousand days later, the prime movers within that complex – the US chiefs of staff, the arms manufacturers, the steel and oil industries – all wanted Kennedy out of office.

His brother's anti-Mafia crusade seemed to the Mob to be against the spirit of an 'agreement' that they later privately claimed they'd brokered with the Kennedys' father during the 1960 election (it's an interesting claim, though why the Kennedys, with 400 million dollars of their own, would want Mafia money is another question entirely). This, combined with the 'loss' of Cuba, was enough to bring the overlapping groups of organised crime and right-wing Cuban exiles into the frame – the latter hand in glove with their CIA sponsors.

Hoover's FBI had been hostile to JFK from the start – and the fact that JFK was not prepared to postpone Hoover's forthcoming retirement date only added to the old man's fury.

The FBI, the CIA, the Mob, the Cuban exiles, Big Business, the Army, the Navy, the Airforce. Even his own Vice President. All wanted Kennedy out of the White House and all were aware that, in the public's eyes, he was as popular as ever, a 'shoo-in' for the 1964 poll (and his brother Bobby 'RFK' Kennedy was surely a racing cert for 1968 and 1972 – the 'unstoppable' FDR ghost, which the Right thought it had firmly buried beneath the Cold War hysteria of the '50s, had returned to haunt them, his torch now borne by the Kennedys).

Kennedy was shot dead at 12:30pm Eastern Standard Time on 22 November 1963. He was hit on Elm Street, Dallas, just past the Dal-Tex Building and Texas Book Depository and to the left of the grassy knoll, which has railway yards behind and beyond it. The Texan Governor Connally was seriously wounded in the attack and a passer-by, one James Tague, received a minor face burn. Kennedy's car windscreen had a bullet hole and other bullets were picked off the ground in the minutes following the killing. Witnesses spoke of four to eight shots and others said there had been 'bursts' of automatic gunfire. Twenty-eight witnesses saw gun smoke or heard gunshots coming from the grassy knoll and several followed at least two Dallas police officers in rushing up the knoll (all were prevented from doing so for a few crucial moments by a man with Secret Service ID – it later turned out to be fake, there were no SS men on the knoll).

Conspiracy theories are ten a penny – many now the subject, often deservedly, of bar-room jokes: 'Elvis Presley's manager killed JFK and Marilyn Monroe before they both moved to the moon?' Yeah, right…

Yet the fact is that people of influence were murdered, were assassinated. And in assassination after assassination, the accepted, official version of events is not just inadequate – it is, time and again, wholly and blatantly wrong. These discrepancies are now so obvious that only the naive, or those with a vested interest, could actually continue to believe them to be wholly innocent. There are few genuine conspiracies, there are even fewer genuine coincidences.

All of the following had some impact, directly and indirectly, on John Lennon's life – and death. In fact, the existence of the penultimate conspiracy herein, the Watergate scandal, cannot be denied by even the most blinkered of commentators – five men working for President Nixon's re-election campaign *did* burgle the Democrat Party HQ at the Watergate Centre in Washington DC. They did so in order to illegally photograph documents, copy files and plant bugs – and they were caught red-handed and arrested on the spot by local police.

It took well over two years but Watergate and the subsequent cover-up did, eventually, force Nixon to resign in shame, sparking half a decade of revelations that were to shock America.

What did not emerge at the time were some other unsavoury connections between Watergate and the, then recent, past. The leader of the Watergate break-in team was Bernard Barker, a CIA 'asset' and former associate of mobster Santos Trafficante. Bernard Barker's two main assistants in planning the Watergate burglary were Frank Sturgis and E Howard Hunt.

During the dying months of 1960 Barker, Hunt and Sturgis had helped General Cabell and Richard Nixon plan the Bay of Pigs attack on Cuba. More disturbing still, Barker himself has been identified by police officer

Seymour Weitzman as being the so-called 'Secret Service agent' who prevented Dallas police officers and others from inspecting the top of the grassy knoll in the seconds after the JFK shooting.

Hunt himself, like Frank Sturgis and David Ferrie, has long been an JFK assassination suspect, and Hunt and Sturgis are believed to be two of the fake tramps arrested in a railway car – and then photographed – behind the grassy knoll within minutes of the 1963 assassination.

One key aspect of the cover-up was the Watergate Tapes – White House recordings of Nixon in conversation with his confederates during 1969–74. There were various unexplained edits and deletions on the tapes, though even the words that were left behind showed that Nixon and Hunt and the other staffers still had, for some strange reason, an incredibly intense interest in the Bay of Pigs fiasco and its 1961–63 aftermath, over a decade after it had happened.

According to E Howard Hunt's biographer, Tad Szulc, Hunt had also been the CIA station chief in Mexico City during September 1963, when an Oswald lookalike had first attempted to create a direct link between JFK's assassination and Cuba and the Soviet Union. Again, it was an overture that the communists suspiciously rejected, the Cuban and Russian embassies refusing to grant visas.

Much of the above was first mentioned in AJ Weberman and Michael Canfield's 1975 book *Coup d'Etat In America; The CIA And The Assassination Of John F Kennedy*, the authors backing their allegation with a CIA memo from an aide to CIA high-up Richard Helms' aide stating that Hunt was in Dallas that day, a memo that showed great concern over the possibility that Hunt's presence there might one day become public knowledge. On publication Hunt immediately tried to sue Weberman and Canfield but when the case finally came to court, his case was quickly thrown out.

In 1985 Marita Lorenz, a former CIA and FBI agent, testified on oath that mercenary Frank Sturgis – her one-time common-law husband – had been one of the men who'd assassinated JFK. She also said that E Howard Hunt and Jack Ruby had visited Sturgis in his Dallas motel room on 21 November 1963, the eve of the assassination, Hunt delivering thousands of dollars in used bills.

According to Lorenz, Sturgis later confessed to his part in the JFK killing. Sturgis himself denied this, though he did admit that he *was* questioned by the FBI over the JFK assassination.

Jack Ruby – an FBI informer, mob associate and former Nixon employee – went on to kill the official assassination suspect, Lee Harvey Oswald, on 24 November 1963, before Oswald could be tried in court.

7 The First Lone Nut

'...we are all puppets...'

– Sirhan Sirhan

On the day of his arrest three Lee Harvey Oswald wallets – two with full ID – were found by the Dallas Police. One was found on Oswald, one was found in his apartment and another wallet was discovered on 10th Street, just a few feet away from where Dallas Police Officer Tippit had been killed.

All of which seems to confirm the theory that it may indeed have been an Oswald lookalike who'd gone round Dallas publicly making anti-American, pro-communist comments in the weeks before the JFK assassination...

Several showgirls from Jack Ruby's Dallas nightclub, the Carousel, later stated that Ruby and Oswald had been 'bedmates' and that assassination suspect David Ferrie had visited the club regularly as well. Oswald had also been in the New Orleans' Civic Air Patrol with Ferrie – a photo has now been unearthed of Oswald and Ferrie at a CAP gathering in 1955 – before joining the US Marines. While there he suffered several mysterious but minor gunshot wounds – one fellow marine said he was faking – and disappeared from barracks for weeks at a time.

When Oswald was in Japan he was based at Atsugi, near Tokyo, a base for America's then secret U-2 spy plane – and a base that was also home to an equally secret stash of H-bombs (officially forbidden on the soil of Japan, the nation that had suffered the first atomic attacks).

Despite having his own apartment and plenty of ready cash from the Carousel Club, Ruby sometimes stayed at the Dallas YMCA, as did

Oswald (the latter on 3 October 1963 and again from 15 October through to 19 October).

Oswald was also described by some of his acquaintances, including former marine colleagues, as being a narcissistic homosexual who was susceptible to hypnosis, '...someone you could brainwash...'.

Oswald's brother Robert, when visiting him at Dallas Police Station the day after he'd allegedly shot JFK, stared into his sibling's eyes looking for any hint of sorrow or conscience. There was zero, 'nothing'. Several Dallas law enforcement officials were later to speak of Oswald's mysterious post-JFK calm in custody, a calmness that – to them at least – suggested deep hypnosis or some kind of 'programming'...

Oswald had left the marines abruptly in 1959 before 'defecting' to the Soviet Union in a rather curious manner – despite officially having virtually no money he'd taken a ship to Britain, then flown on to the Finnish capital Helsinki (where he stayed in an upmarket hotel) and then entered the Soviet Union using a one-week tourist visa and the most expensive means of transport possible (a trip that would have cost him, in today's terms, anything up to 8,000 or 9,000 dollars).

Once there, delays led him to attempt suicide in order to persuade the Soviets he was serious; an act of self-harm that his new Russian doctor Lydia Mikhailina did not believe was serious. Seven months after his defection the Russians downed a USAF spy plane, Gary Powers' U-2 jet, over Soviet territory.

Although the 1 May 1960 spy plane incident seemed to be an embarrassing setback for America – at 90,000 feet the U-2 had been thought to be untouchable – it was paradoxically greeted with joy by both the US military chiefs of staff and the CIA. Both groups had felt that US President 'Ike' Eisenhower was getting too friendly with the Soviet's moderate post-Stalin leader Khrushchev and the U-2 setback caused immense damage to relations between the two men – it happened just before an important summit meeting.

A few months after the U-2 episode, Oswald, who'd never been fully trusted or accepted by his Soviet handlers, 'defected back' to the USA – incredibly there remains no record of any attempt at a debriefing by either the CIA or FBI (not even when Oswald's interest in cameras led him to a job with the Jaggars Chiles Stovall Company, a firm doing top-secret photographic work for the US government).

Oswald did, however, later get in touch with Dallas FBI agent James P Hosty Jr, but Oswald's last pre-assassination note to Hosty was destroyed in late November 1963 on the orders of local FBI office chief J Gordon Shanklin.

One of the other main problems with the official 'Oswald was a commie' theory was Oswald's pro-Castro Fair Play For Cuba leaflets. Many of them initially had a New Orleans address stamped on the back, an address – 544 Camp Street – that was linked to both US Naval Intelligence and anti-Castro gunmen as well as assassination suspects Guy Banister, David Ferrie and Clay Shaw (Shaw was taken to court in 1967 by New Orleans DA Jim Garrison, a case that was the basis for Oliver Stone's 1992 film *JFK* – in reality Banister died of an alleged 'heart attack' within ten days of the last Warren Commission hearing while Ferrie, who told friends he'd 'never' commit suicide, was found dead with a suicide note before he could testify in New Orleans; Shaw himself was eventually acquitted, partly because most other American states refused to extradite witnesses to New Orleans...).

Anyone who's seriously studied the Oswald evidence rapidly comes to several contradictory conclusions about the man – recent revelations, however, now make it easier to establish some sort of coherent whole.

Oswald started to work with the CIA after joining the marines in 1959 – he'd been groomed for the role by gay right-wing mentors like CAP volunteer David Ferrie, a devotee of the Rev George A Hyde of the Orthodox Catholic Church. The Agency was already 'running' a passable Oswald lookalike when the 'original' was still in his mid teens (this accounts for the innumerable discrepancies between the short, shy Harvey Oswald schoolboy from Yorkville, New York, and the pushier, taller southern boy Lee Oswald from New Orleans – it also explains how, when Oswald was in Russia, Lee Oswald could simultaneously be seen attempting to buy trucks or guns in New Orleans, how Oswald could be seen in the USA at the same time as another 'Oswald' was making waves in Mexico City – an 'Oswald' who, according to young Mexican radicals, was obviously not the leftist he claimed to be).

Using such young people was not so new in the spook world – Britain's Royal Navy spy Christopher Creighton, aka John Ainsworth Davis, claimed to have been groomed and recruited when he was barely 16 years old and the Soviets had a phrase that summed up their young 'sleeper' schemes: 'wine-cask fill', which basically meant new wine in old bottles (an identity built on a fading, faked, photo from the Raj or pre-war Paris could be combined with a forged ID and soon a teenage graduate of the Minsk spy school would be starting a new life in Europe, Asia or America, trained to put up an endless front, trained to observe and wait years if necessary, all the time holding on for the call).

Oswald, a confused homosexual in an age when such a lifestyle was both 'shameful' and illegal, voluntarily underwent deep hypnosis as he got further into the US foreign intelligence services – US Naval Intelligence and liaisons with the CIA. The alter ego that emerged after such hypnotic sessions is no longer gay but heterosexual instead, sometimes aggressively so – a ladies' man, a 'programmed' ladies' man. During his various fake-injury recovery periods, the US 'Marine Oswald' learned Russian and a few more of the U-2 spy secrets – these he was to give to the Russians in order to widen the gap between the US and Soviet leadership.

After the US U-2 project was betrayed, Oswald had another secret mission in Russia (after he'd been photographed a few times by US tourists who just happened to be in the same parts of Russia). That mission was to try and lure the daughter of a KGB high-up, a man connected to the Minsk spy school, to the West – with her father soon to follow.

Marina Pruskakova was intrigued by Oswald's move – as was the KGB who were soon briefing Marina. They allowed her to marry Oswald and even let the couple leave for America (there were no real secrets beyond the U-2 spy plane that Oswald had ever been privy to).

Back in the USA, the CIA – in conjunction with the FBI – arranged for Oswald to infiltrate and subvert the pro-Castro Fair Play For Cuba movement. The ultimate aim was to destroy it, of course. Oswald gave out pro-Cuban leaflets – quickly scrubbing out the Camp Street address after he noticed it – and engaged in fake fights and media debates which he knew he would lose (because his primed opponents knew they could always drop the 'he's a defector to Russia' bombshell).

Whenever Oswald got into real trouble, he amazed local police by summoning the FBI, who'd always get him released within minutes (hardly the service they'd render a real 'Red'). He made friends, secretly, with Dallas Police Officer Tippit and got reacquainted with Jack Ruby, who also seemed to know Tippit.

At the same time, the other, taller, tougher 'Oswald' was creating quite a stir with his outrageous anti-American remarks – he also placed orders for guns through mail order (something quite unnecessary then in Dallas, since any kind of gun could have been bought over the counter for cash by anyone over 18 – but mail-order receipts do leave a nice trail to the quieter Harvey Oswald).

As the day of JFK's assassination moved closer, those who were in on it within the CIA heirachy coordinated their own Agency-mob 'shooter team' as well as backups from Cuba and the Middle East. Trusted elements within the FBI and US Military Intelligence – and, of course, the military-industrial complex – were more than happy to cooperate.

Hoover got the warnings – including the 17 November 1963 FBI memo giving notice that a 'MILITANT REVOLUTIONARY GROUP MAY ATTEMPT TO ASSASSINATE PRESIDENT KENNEDY ON HIS PROPOSED TRIP TO DALLAS, TEXAS, 11-22-63' – and ignored them completely. The shooters who were important enough to be interested were told that, with Kennedy dead, Cuba could be won back and Communist Vietnam liberated. If that damaged East–West relationships, so much the better. If it even provoked all-out war with the Soviets then so be it – better now than later when the Soviets would be stronger...

A few weeks before the assassination, the quiet but arrogant Harvey Oswald was told that his next assignment was to help expose shortcomings within the US Secret Service – when Kennedy visited Dallas a shot was to be fired close to the President. The subsequent shake-up would improve the Secret Service's presidential protection squad.

On 22 November, the unwitting Harvey Oswald went to work – making no attempt at disguise or subterfuge – and allowed three men, including one dark-skinned Cuban, into the Texas Book Depository (other gunmen lurked in the Dal-Tex building, on the grassy knoll, in the Elm Street storm drains...).

As the clocks strike 12:30pm. President Kennedy's Lincoln, 'Lancer', turns into Elm Street and slowly starts to straighten up – a perfect target. A single shot shatters the silence. It is followed two seconds later by a series of shots from a Mauser rifle and two new automatic rifles – M1 or prototype M-16s – fitted with silencers.

They pepper the presidential Lincoln and the area around it – a bullet flies down the triple underpass, as another sends concrete chips of sidewalk up into the air. Others hit human targets.

All the while the shooters' radio coordinator on the ground barks 'Shoot! Shoot! Shoot!' into his mini-radio mic as an umbrella flaps up and down beside him. Then, amazingly, 'Lancer' – against all the rules of presidential driving – slowed to a virtual halt. An even easier target.

Of the 15-plus Secret Servicemen in the JFK motorcade only three made any move to help the President. The shots continued to slam in from left and right as the SS men behind the car twitched hopelessly.

One TV reporter described the shots as being three 'bursts' of automatic gunfire, and dozens of other witnesses recall hearing four or more shots. Even many of those who only hear three shots testify that they were not evenly spaced (later to be a key issue).

Governor Connally is seriously wounded, the Lincoln's windscreen gets a hole, passer-by James Tague gets away with a cut cheek – and then, after eight seconds of mayhem, Kennedy finally has the back of his head blown away. The fatal shot comes from the front, on the right, piercing Kennedy's right temple, shattering the back of his skull and splashing his wife with brain and bone.

With Kennedy's head open and parts of his brain in his wife's lap, the blood-splattered wife, Jackie, is torn between two awful choices: the agony of holding her dying husband...or trying to survive herself by climbing out of a car that's still being hit.

After almost seven seconds of slowing down and with Kennedy now seriously hit, 'Lancer' finally started to accelerate away, as an SS man leapt uselessly on the back bonnet. Did the SS man help Mrs Kennedy stay in the car, or is it her that prevented him from falling off as the Lincoln gathered speed? It doesn't matter, the gunshots had at last stopped with the police sirens drowning out the screams.

The 35th president of the United States, fatally wounded, is just minutes away from death...

Angry passers-by joined motorcycle cops in running to where over 25 people have seen gun smoke or heard gunshots – up on the grassy knoll. Bernard Barker used his fake Secret Service ID to turn most of them away.

Seconds later the news filtered down to Oswald, still on one of the Book Depository's lower floors. He been half expecting the first shot – this was surely the Secret Service security test his handlers had warned him about – but as the other explosive sounds continued to penetrate the quiet of the book warehouse he knew something had gone awfully, fatally wrong.

Within seconds he knows that Kennedy has been shot, that Kennedy is seriously wounded – 'No, No,' says someone with a good view of the last, fatal head shot from the knoll, 'President Kennedy is dying!'

By 12:33pm the news is on the wires but those hoping to get confirmation direct from Washington DC are disappointed – no one can get through, the entire DC phone network has been sabotaged.

Halfway across the country, one of the Latino maids looking after JFK's children is said to have remembered the military *coup d'états* in her own country and starts to dress the youngsters for a quick getaway.

Eight miles above the mid-Pacific, en route to Vietnam, Kennedy's cabinet see a ticker-tape message announcing that JFK has been 'seriously wounded' in Dallas. They try to use code to contact Washington DC but the presidential code book is missing. The US government is completely stranded, unable to contact Washington and with their current peace mission to Vietnam now rendered meaningless...

Oswald at last realises what the hypnosis sessions – and his in-built sense of superiority – have kept from him. He – the 'pro-Castro commie', the Red who came back from Russia – is the fall guy, the patsy, *the kid in the frame. There was no Secret Service readiness test.*

He tries to remember the emergency plan, the backup in case anything ever went wrong – Tippit, the .38, the one-two beep, the shirt, the out-of-town airfield. Oswald goes to leave the Depository – two cops stop him but quickly let him go: he isn't even sweating, they quite rightly reason, how can he have run down from the 6th floor where the shots are supposed to have come from?

Oswald gets back to his new apartment in time for his landlady to witness Tippit's cop car pulling up outside – the cop car beeps its horn twice then moves slowly forwards. Oswald goes to his bedroom, grabs the .38 handgun and the police shirt that he hopes will get him out of town (the shirt's probably unnecessary, he only brings it in case Tippit's forgotten his spare police shirt, all part of the backup plan).

Oswald hurries down 10th Street to see a horrifying sight – Tippit is with another man, the latter points at Harvey Oswald, urges Tippit on. Tippit is part of it too. *Tippit is supposed to kill him! The so-called commie, the fleeing assassin. Oswald. Kill Him!*

Fighting back a wave of nausea, Oswald spins on his heels and starts to run-walk off down a side street – he glances back as the CIA op runs out of patience and actually shoots Tippit, *kills Tippit on the spot* (later the spare police shirt will be found in the back of Tippit's squad car – no official explanation is ever offered).

Oswald sees the operative drop something on the ground near Tippit but by now he's running too hard to think. The Texas Theater and Ruby. That's his last and only hope.

It's not until Oswald is within sight of the Texas Theater cinema that he recalls the obvious – the CIA operative with the gun looked a little like himself. Just a little. Like himself. He's to be framed for Tippit's killing too.

Although this is Dallas, where half the cops are Ku Klux Klan supporters who hate Kennedy, the embarrassment of 'losing' the president is now compounded by the very real police anger that surrounds the killing of a cop. No one's hit a Dallas cop for over a dozen years – *that must be part of the plan too, it's so obvious now, Oswald's not going to be taken alive.*

He charges into the Texas Theater – buy a ticket? are you kidding? – and prays that this contact, this last sole contact, will be true. Will not just sit there up in the balcony.

But within moments the electric whine of the DPD tells another, more bitter tale – there's no one trying to contact him. He's to die alone…but as the nanoseconds turn into seconds into moments into minutes – or what seem like minutes – Harvey Oswald realises that they're waiting. The cops and the FBI and the Agency and the Secret Service. All just waiting. Where's Jack? Where's Ruby?

The obvious thing to do is just run out of the back fire exit – but that's *too* obvious, that's where they're waiting, he knows there'll be half a dozen gunmen round the back – he'd be dead within seconds, without witnesses. Killed while trying to escape.

No, no, make them do it here. Make them blow me away in front of all these teenagers and housewives, right here in the movie theatre.

Suddenly the house lights start coming up and several cops, guns drawn, begin to wander cautiously down the aisles. Why haven't they come in in force? *Because this way you might just get a chance to hurt another cop and then they'll definitely waste you; that way you'll definitely never live to see the cop shop, let alone a court of law. That's why they're sending in a trickle of cannon fodder, bit by bit.*

But there's just a glimpse of daylight through the tired drapes behind one of the cops. By the entrance. A flicker of hope. He might just be able to make a run for it, back into the street and grab a car and run. But where to? A cop eyeballs him, turns away but keeps moving in roughly the same direction, closer, closer. Another flicker of daylight hope through the drapes, drapes like at a funeral parlour – Oswald grips the .38 in his sweating hand as the nervous couple each side of him start to scramble away. *Ohmigod! Ohmigod!*

Harvey Oswald leaps up, knows he can't get past the nearest cop without shooting – he aims and fires but the only sound is a hollow click.

Click! Click! Click! The .38 is useless. *They've been in his apartment, they've sawn the hammer off. It doesn't matter.* The .38 is useless. The trap is complete.

Struggling with the cop, two more closing in – none of them firing. Stricken faces of the kids in the tip-up seats, backing off – all good clean skinny, chubby, Americans. *All looking shocked – not enjoying the show that's there for their benefit.*

Struggling with the cops, Oswald takes two more punches, but they're not, it seems, going to kill him. Not here. As the marks start to squeeze out of the side fire exits – kids playing truant, housewives holding the wrong man's hand, guilty witnesses leaving the scene of the future crime – the wanted man sees he has to make a fuss or he might still die where he stands. A shotgun butt smashes into his back. He suddenly shouts: 'I must protest this police brutality! *Police Brutality!*'

A couple of the marks slow down, turn and look back. The useless gun is taken from Oswald, he's turned and cuffed. Bastard killed an officer – slap, *slap*. *Are you sure?* No, but one of the motorcycle officers said so.

It's still midday, not even two. An hour and a half ago Oswald was still playing the semi-retired spy, serving the red, white and blue to the best of his ability. *Now what?* The words come back into his head – calmness, *Lee, calmness, there is nothing to be afraid of, your father's gone, there's nothing to be afraid of, there's just calmness, calmness, calmness.*

Within seconds Oswald's smiling again, albeit feebly, half-lost in his self-induced world. As they push his head down to get him into the police car's back seat, Oswald glances up and back at the Texas Theater – through the glass double doors he sees the drapes being pushed asunder. He looks back around him – six, seven, eight police cars. *Calmness. The name of the lawyer to ask for is Abt. John Abt. John Abt.*

His eyes count the police cars again. *Two, four, six, eight.*

There's safety in repetition. Calmness, calmness, calmness...the internal tranquillity is balanced with fear and sadness. He doesn't know why. *His life's been a lie since he was 14.* The northerner playing a southerner, the second-generation German-American with the Polish accent. The 'happily married' man who can only make love when he's programmed to – and that with a woman he still half suspects is a KGB junior. Now with child – a true Cold War family. With daddy under arrest.

And he still doesn't know why, a bit-part patsy in his own life story. He's achieved calm but somehow there is still...

Sadness, *calmness.* Now everyone will know who I really am...*it'll all come out – the U-2 betrayal, the FBI meets, the YMCA circuit, the gay sessions, the Cuban fakery* – but some of those weren't his fault, some of those were orders. *Calmness* – but now everyone will know who

I really am – no longer under cover...*calmness, calmness, calmness.* He realises someone is speaking. It's all going to come out. Lee Harvey Oswald looks up at the Dallas detective and smiles sadly.

'Now everyone will know who I am.'

As the Texas Theater curtains flap open, Ruby steps out into the foyer his teeth already chewing his bottom lip as he watches Harvey Oswald's own little motorcade scream away.

'We didn't get him,' Ruby thinks, over and over, 'We just didn't get him. What the hell went wrong?' Muttering obscenities, Ruby gets in the big car, 1958 vintage, as his driver puts it in gear.

Within hours of the JFK assassination word of Oswald's 'communist' links had begun to leak out. Phase One, in CIA parlance, begins. The story of the 'Red Sniper'. If any low-level cop or FBI agent starts to seriously investigate Oswald's background – and discovers the fake nature of his so-called Marxism – then the Agency will shift its press and police contacts towards Phase Two.

Phase Two is the 'Lone Nut' theory. This is even less believable than the 'Red Sniper' theory but it is backed up with the threat of real fear. The inquisitive will be told that if an investigation goes any further then the serious depth of Oswald's communist roots will be revealed, resulting in a nuclear war with Russia. Phase Two will be supported by a commission of inquiry of 'impeccable integrity'.

If and when Phases One and Two fall apart then Phase Three of the cover-up stands ready – years later – to give out a few clues that will lead everyone to blame those who were merely the help, the gun help. Blame it all on the Mob.

Of course, all these cover-up levels, these phases, depend on one thing – that there will be no trial, that Oswald will be killed while being arrested.

After 24 hours of almost non-stop interrogation – for which no tapes are used and no shorthand notes taken – the Dallas Police prepare to transfer Oswald to the county jail. As his wallet and ID – well, one set of them anyway – have been found near Officer Tippit's body, Oswald's already been charged with that murder.

He is to be transferred through the basement where the world's press, now in a feeding frenzy, waits for him.

In the basement, one cop lets Ruby in through a side door as another shelters him from the impatient cameras of the press. Although no one knows it yet, Ruby has already been accidentally snapped near Elm Street, just a stone's throw from both the grassy knoll and the Texas Book Depository, and at Parkland Hospital as JFK died, and then at a police press conference (it's Ruby who hastily dives in when a police spokesman links Oswald with the Free Cuba movement, 'It's Fair Play For Cuba,' he shouts, worried lest anyone should get the wrong – or rather the right – idea). Ruby's on-oath claim, that he was an apolitical person who decided to kill Oswald that morning purely to save Jackie Kennedy the hassle of going before court, simply does not hold water.

Oswald's last recorded words, delivered over his shoulder as he's led away from the last brief question-and-answer session, are almost a scream: 'I'm just a patsy!'

Now dressed in sober black jersey and white shirt, Oswald comes out of the lift – a little wired but, in the circumstances, he's actually quite calm, calmer than anyone else in the room.

It's 11:21am and Oswald is brought forward slowly – too slowly but that's inevitable since the 1963 Ford Galaxie that's supposed to be whisking him away is backing up towards him at far too leisurely a pace.

As he wonders if the car's slothfulness is deliberate, Oswald approaches the crescent of pressmen. A familiar face – Jack Ruby's – appears from behind the sheltering police officer. Oswald goes to give a half smile but before the expression even reaches his face it goes into reverse. Ruby is rapidly raising a handgun. As a shocked Oswald cringes, Ruby fires a single shot into his abdomen.

Ruby is instantly dragged to the ground and arrested – 'What did you do that for, Jack?' allegedly asks one cop who's more irritated than annoyed. Everyone at the station knows Jack Ruby, they've all drunk in his strip club.

A police officer leans on the stricken Oswald's abdomen and starts giving him artificial respiration, the worst possible treatment for an abdominal gunshot wound.

An ambulance is on the scene with suspicious speed. Barely 90 seconds after Ruby's pulled the trigger, the medical team begin to drive down into the basement. Before 11:30am – less than nine minutes after the shooting – they have Oswald in Parkland where, in under two hours, he's dead.

Vice President Johnson has already been sworn in as the new US President, Jackie Kennedy by his side, her pink Chanel suit now caked with blood. Johnson's elevation to the presidency means he can now avoid the Estes and Bobby Baker financial scandals that could have put him in jail – no wonder at least one photo taken later that day shows him smiling. His first two major actions are straightforward. He cancels Kennedy's memo NSAM 263 pulling US troops out of Vietnam and instead sends more (within three years he will pour over a quarter of a million US troops into Vietnam).

And then LBJ tells a grinning Hoover that he won't be forced to resign his FBI directorship the next year.

As questions continue to be asked over the JFK assassination, Johnson sets up the Warren Commission to investigate – its panel includes right-wing Republican Gerald Ford and former CIA director Allen W Dulles, the man who JFK had fired over the Bay of Pigs fiasco. By the time they first meet, the leftist Fair Play For Cuba committee is history, having been forced out of business by its faint but controversial link with 'volunteer' Lee Harvey Oswald.

In late 1964 the Warren Commission announces its verdict – it has decided that Lee Harvey Oswald was JFK's sole assassin, committing the killing from the sixth floor of the Texas Book Depository.

Using one second-rate rifle and firing three evenly spaced bullets, Oswald had hit Kennedy's neck before wounding Governor Connally and then finally killing JFK with a headshot.

This miracle of solo marksmanship was accomplished against a moving target, in under 4.6 seconds and from a distance of over 130 feet – and all done with a 20-year-old weapon that was in such poor condition FBI riflemen later refused to test fire it until a complete barrel rebore had been performed.

The ammo round that wounded Connally has since become known as the 'magic bullet' as, in order to hit JFK in the back, exit upwardly through his neck and then go on through to wound Connally the bullet must have changed directions several times both before and after hitting the governor. To compound the 'magic', the bullet in question is found in virtually mint condition. Its discovery is similarly unreal – it is found on Connally's previously clean hospital stretcher.

The Warren Commission ignored the possibility that the 'magic bullet' was in such good condition purely because it hadn't hit anyone (that would mean there were more than three shots fired and any more than three means there must have been a second gunman).

The Warren Commission ignored the slight wound suffered by passer-by James Tague (that would again suggest that there were more than three shots fired).

The Warren Commission ignored the photos of FBI and Secret Servicemen picking up bullets from the roadside (that would again mean there were more than three shots fired).

The Warren Commission ignored the bullet hole in the presidential Lincoln's windscreen (that would again mean there were more than three shots fired).

The Warren Commission ignored the several witnesses who heard bursts of gunfire, suggesting at least one automatic weapon (that would again mean there were more than three shots fired).

The Warren Commission ignored the witnesses who heard four or more gunshots (that would again mean there were more than three shots fired).

The Warren Commission ignored the 28 witnesses who heard gunshots, or saw gunsmoke, coming from the grassy knoll (that would again mean there were more than three shots fired).

The Warren Commission accepted the FBI and CIA statements – since proved false – that they had had no contact with Oswald in the months before the assassination.

The Warren Commission ignored the numerous witnesses who'd seen Oswald with Ruby before the assassination.

The Warren Commission ignored the fact that Oswald's 'work' for the Fair Play For Cuba Committee had been patently designed to discredit the FPCC – Oswald's actions were actually anti-leftist, something else the Commission chose to turn a blind eye to.

In defiance of all the above facts – and many others too numerous to chronicle in a single volume – the Warren Commission blandly concluded that Oswald had acted alone, in complete isolation. The quiet, sometimes shy, Oswald killed the President purely to seek attention. Oswald is dubbed the 'lone nut'.

The resulting Warren Report is now seen as a complete whitewash by virtually all serious assassination researchers (public scepticism has grown too – currently over 90 per cent of the American public disbelieve the report).

For anyone who still believes in official government denials, 'lone nuts', 'commie agents' and 'magic bullets', here is one simple statistic. Between the winters of 1963 and 1967, 15 JFK assassination witnesses who'd been interviewed by the Warren Commission, the Dallas Police or the FBI died prematurely – the causes of death were a bizarre blend of gunshots, hit-and-run car crashes, highway accidents, unexpected suicides, heart attacks, cut throats and karate chops.

When *The Sunday Times* got an actuary to compute the life expectancy of the dead witnesses – he concluded that the odds, on 22 November 1963, against all 15 of them being dead before February 1967 were over one hundred thousand trillion to one. Or, to put it numerically, in excess of 100,000,000,000,000,000 to 1.

By the time the actuary had finished his calculations, four more JFK witnesses were dead...

US Army intelligence destroyed their file on Lee Harvey Oswald in 1973; this was done, they claimed, purely for routine, 'space-saving' reasons. Despite the 1977–79 House Committee on Assassinations, despite the 1966 Freedom of Information Act – and its 1974 amendments – and despite the 1992 JFK Act...the awful truth is that we have to try and work with what we've got, for the CIA files on JFK, RFK, Martin Luther King, Malcolm X and John Lennon remain incomplete and, for the most part, unseen.

Just as hard to believe is the fact that, to this day, the engraved motto outside the CIA's HQ remains the biblical quote, 'And the truth will set you free...'

8 Invasion!

'The Beatles were always supposing they were Smokey Robinson.'
— *John Lennon*

On 9 February 1964, The Beatles, then Number One on both sides of the Atlantic made their first live appearance on American television. The *Ed Sullivan Show* was watched by a staggering 73 million viewers that night and crime levels dipped to their lowest in years as everyone from bank managers to car thieves decided to check out the latest musical sensation from the England.

Though the media culture vultures mostly sneered – *The New York Times* critic found the boys 'incoherent...schematic' – within days The Beatles were holding the top five chart spots in the US, a feat never before – or since – matched.

There are a hundred reasons why The Beatles got so big so fast in the US – talent not being the least of them – but timing was a big part of it too. A stunned America was still mourning the death of JFK less than three months before – and The Beatles were, for young people at least, the perfect way to lift the gloom. They were young, hip, energetic, witty *and* foreign, while still speaking English. They offered something a bit more raw than the usual pop pap. They had a certain honesty and even their detractors admitted they also had humour.

Reporter:	Will you sing something for us now?
JL:	We need cash first.
Reporter:	How would you account for your success?
JL:	We've got a good press agent.

2nd reporter:	When do you rehearse?
JL:	We don't.
PMc:	Yeah, of course we do.
JL:	Paul does, we don't.
3rd reporter:	But surely you don't need all this police protection? Surely you can handle it all yourselves?
JL:	Maybe you can, you're a lot fatter than we are...

Everyone from radical beat poet Allen Ginsberg to teenage cheerleaders to an 11-year-old Nile Rodgers fell for the Fab Four magic. ('Yeah, I dug The Beatles, the thing is Afro hair just don't shake like that,' said Rodgers, the co-founder of Chic and one-time Bowie producer, 'so when I wanted to do that shaking moptop thing I'd put my running shorts on my head, grab my tennis racket guitar and then start shaking my ass off!')

They were a sensation, with Brian Epstein making tens of thousands of dollars – and losing millions more – on merchandising as Beatle toys, wigs, lunch boxes, posters, jeans, boots, jackets, T-shirts, handbags, sweets and cakes swamped America.

According to legend, Epstein nearly cost the band even more than that. Within hours of arriving in the US, jet-lagged and hungover, he'd done something he wouldn't have ever dared do back in Britain – he'd picked up a boy in his late teens, straight off the street. Having whisked his 'rough trade' back to his hotel, Epstein was about to consummate the 'relationship' when a faint motorised whirring could be heard. A photographer, trying to stalk The Beatles from a fire escape, had instead grabbed a shot of Epstein doing something that was illegal in 38 states – including New York. There were many industry people hoping the Fabbies would fail and Epstein's outrage, if it had ever become public, might just have led to that happening.

Luckily for him, after he'd scrambled to the phone, Capitol had staffers on the case within seconds. Minutes later a photographer was manhandled on the doorstep of his apartment and had his film stolen – $2,000 cash was slapped in his hand as compensation for his 'time and trouble'. He was then told to just forget all he'd seen that day – to forget it or risk being sued. Apparently the photographer *has* forgotten it because, even up to this very day, the photographer – if he ever existed – has maintained a dignified silence.

Between the first and second visits to America came *A Hard Day's Night*, The Beatles' movie debut with a Lennon theme song and much frantic direction from Dick Lester. The story – The Beatles under siege, the 'car, then a room then another car' lifestyle of pop stardom – was basic enough but the fresh performances and the driving soundtrack gave it something more. Only the last reel – an adequately filmed piece of concert miming – slows things down and even then the fast-cutting end titles finish things on a high.

During the filming Lennon got to know, and like, actors Victor Spinetti and Eleanor Brown, friendships that would last. *A Hard Day's Night* was, however, still shot in black and white. Although The Beatles had sold millions they were still regarded by United Artists Films as being a bit of a risk – *any of these pop bands could completely fade away at any minute, couldn't they? It's all just a short-lived fad, isn't it...?*

The Beatles first 'proper' American tour came in August 1964, covering two dozen cities coast to coast during 34 hectic days. It was a triumphant series of concerts despite receiving bomb threats in Las Vegas – possibly over Lennon's public refusal to play southern gigs where the audience would be 'segregated and black people have to sit at the back, we've never played segregated gigs and we're not gonna start now' (John's comments were relevant internationally too for 1964 was also the year that the CIA policy of shopping the 'dangerous communist terrorist' Nelson Mandela to the South African police paid off – he was sentenced to life imprisonment on Robbin Island).

In Kansas The Beatles had played for $150,000, a million pounds today, a record fee of almost $5,000 dollars a minute. By the following Easter, The Beatles accounted for over 85 per cent of all American single sales of the previous year.

After returning to the UK, Lennon casually helped save the career of comedian and writer Peter Cook. Dudley Moore's comic partner had returned from New York after losing thousands on a Broadway show that flopped. With no offers on the table – and the satirical show *That Was The Week That Was* off the air because of the UK election – Cook found himself near bankruptcy. When Moore, a talented piano player in his own right, got his own one-off BBC show he was told that Cook could only appear as part of an all-star line up. If such a thing could be found.

Lennon heard the news, volunteered instantly and did two sketches for a show that got rave reviews. The 'one-off' quickly morphed into the long-running *Not Only But Also* series, making household names of Cook and Moore.

In Britain the neo-socialist Labour Party won the general election, ending 13 years of Tory rule and making Harold Wilson prime minister. On the same day, 16 October, Red China exploded its first h-bomb. In Russia, the Communist Party decided that with the Americans killing off their liberal leader, JFK, the Soviet Union no longer needed its own and Khrushchev was forced into a *dacha* and early retirement.

Glasnost was postponed for over 20 years as the more militaristic Brezhnev became the effective leader of the USSR. He increased ICBM production at the behest of the Red Army. News of which, when combined with China's h-bomb test, gave the world balance of power a subtle shift. A nuclear war no longer seemed so winnable or so desirable for most of America's hawks – a reasonable notion that managed to last for a decade and a half.

The hawks' own political frontman, Republican presidential candidate Barry Goldwater, had gone into that November's US election with the slogan 'Goldwater: In Your Heart You Know He's Right!' Goldwater had once threatened to use 'small scale' tactical h-bombs in Vietnam and President Johnson's Democrat supporters swiftly responded with the most devastating TV advert in electoral history – 'Daisy Girl' – wherein a small child picks the petals off a daisy in a kind of countdown. In the last few seconds of the ad the child is shockingly bleached out while the picture becomes an atomic explosion as Goldwater's boast is twisted against him: 'In Your Heart You Know He Might!' (young Democrats later came up with an even crueller parody: 'Goldwater: In Your Guts You Know He's Nuts!').

Not surprisingly Johnson won the election with the biggest landslide ever seen in US history. The Democrats also took both Houses of Congress and the majority of governorships...

The second Beatles feature film, 1965's *Help!*, was a colour extravaganza that involved endless set changes and jet-setting. It also had another Lennon theme song that, like 'A Hard Day's Night', was taken as being lyrically something of a humorous number. Why would wildly successful John Lennon ever want help?

Yet Lennon did want help, for he *was* worried about his weight, his songwriting, his direction, his marriage. Cooped up in his big new house in the stockbroker town of Weybridge, Lennon felt torn between the city's bright lights, the experiences he should still be seeking out...and guilt over the beautiful wife and young boy-child he'd already neglected far too much.

9 Under Fire

'Burn The Beatles!'

– Memphis banner

As The Beatles arrived in the Philippines on 3 July 1966, *The New York Times* ran a Lennon quote about how show business was 'an extension of the Jewish religion'. Despite some muttering, in a less politically correct age this comment was accepted without serious criticism.

But three weeks later – after riots at both Japanese and Filipino gigs – *Datebook*, a US magazine aimed at high-school teens, finally ran the Maureen Cleeve *Evening Standard* interview, which she'd conducted with John – now John Lennon OBE – some four months previously. *Datebook* ran it as a front-page story with, of course, Lennon's sensational remarks on religion to the fore.

> 'Christianity will go, it will vanish and shrink. I needn't argue with that; I'm right and I will be proved right. We are more popular than Jesus now; I don't know which'll go first, rock 'n' roll or Christianity. Jesus was alright but his disciples were thick and ordinary. It's them twisting it that ruins it for me.'

In 58 casually spoken words Lennon had sparked a controversy that would plague him and The Beatles for the rest of their careers Stateside – for Lennon the same words would haunt him for the rest of his life. They would even, some claimed, play a role in his death. For what looked like Lennon being his usual opinionated self in Britain, played like blasphemous arrogance in the US, especially the Deep South where Christian churches often tended to be run by, and for, fundamentalists.

In Alabama there were 'Beatle-burning' rallies at which thousands of the groups' records were publicly torched. Dozens of other similar events spread across the south and 30 radio stations banished The Beatles from the airwaves. As the Vatican complained about 'beatniks' dealing in 'profanity', worries grew about security for the forthcoming Fab Four tour of the US. The fact that the group's next single, released just a few days later, was the McCartney-dominated 'Eleanor Rigby' – with lines about a lonely priest failing to 'save' anyone – only made matters worse.

John's remarks were also, though no one said so publicly at the time, a chance for US pundits to vent their growing resentment of the 'British invasion' and the scruffy foreigners who'd spearheaded it since early 1964. Music and film were, are, billion-dollar industries in the US, major exports that local professionals will defend vigorously. When big money is threatened it can often react aggressively, sometimes even with violence.

For instance, some five years later, one of the Jackson Five, then at the height of their teenybopper fame, began to 'go steady' with a particular girl, something that could have threatened the boys' 'young, free and single' image if it had become public knowledge. When the Jacksons' father asked a record executive what could be done about the girl he was instantly told that a fatal 'accident' could quickly be arranged for her. Jackson Senior reacted with revulsion, angrily rejecting the idea and subsequently nothing happened to the girl in question. But such an episode does show how much more seriously such things are taken in the US.

The Beatles' US record label, Capitol, took Lennon's Jesus remarks seriously in August 1966 – it had no choice as talk of bans and boycotts spread across the country. On 6 August Brian Epstein had told the New York press that 'John Lennon's views have been misrepresented...displayed out of context.'

It wasn't enough – two days later, as the US radio blacklist grew to 35 major stations, all Beatles and John Lennon records were banned from South African airwaves (a ban that, in Lennon's case, held until his death 14 years later).

As the US tour grew ever closer Lennon himself still stood by most of his words and he told Epstein he'd rather the gigs be cancelled than have to fully withdraw the remarks. After much persuasion it was decided that Lennon would make some sort of clarification-cum-apology at a pre-tour press conference in Chicago on 11 August.

By this point Lennon was willing to offer some sort of apology but the seriousness of the event was only just beginning to dawn on him. Beforehand, press officer Tony Barrow told him to expect outright hostility as Epstein finally expressed his fear that the tour, without a sincere apology, could end with both Lennon and the entire band being assassinated. But both Barrow and Epstein were still astonished to see, for the first and last time, tears in Lennon's eyes. Almost sobbing at the thought of endangering the others, John told them he'd do 'anything' to make matters right.

The following Astor Towers Hotel press conference was tense from the start – as the band arrived the journalists at the front were told to 'kneel for The Beatles', an accidental 'blasphemy' of the organisers' that was said purely to allow photographers at the back to get a chance to see the group.

After saying that he might have got away with saying 'television is more popular than Jesus', Lennon stumblingly added, 'I used the word "Beatles" as a remote thing, not as what I think. Not as Beatles, as those other Beatles like other people see us. I just said "they" are having more influence on kids and things than anything else, including Jesus...I'm not saying we're better or greater or comparing us with Jesus Christ as a person or God as a thing or whatever it is. I just said what I said and it was wrong. Or it was taken wrong.'

But, a DJ demanded, are you actually prepared to apologise? Lennon tried to clarify things further. 'I'm not anti-God, anti-Christ or anti-religion... I believe in God but not as an old man in the sky.' He then added words that were almost Buddhist in their simplicity and meaning, 'I believe what people call God is something in all of us.'

The press circus ended with Lennon being as blatant, and as irritated, as circumstance allowed – 'I'm sorry I said it really, I never meant it to be a lousy anti-religious thing. I apologise if that will make you happy. I still don't know quite what I've done. I've tried to tell you what I did do but if you want me to apologise, if that will make you happy, then okay, I'm sorry.'

If was enough, just, to satisfy most of the media – and most of the American public. The tour went ahead although the Louisville, Kentucky, concert was cancelled and, at the Washington DC gig, Ku Klux Klan members staged a noisy demonstration outside.

Worse was to come when the band finally played a southern venue, the Mid-South Coliseum in Memphis, on 19 August. The band started well enough, despite record-burning sessions from WAAX radio, anonymous death threats and a promise from the local KKK chapter that there would be a reception The Beatles 'would never forget'.

But halfway through, a gunshot rang out amid the girlish screams and The Beatles looked anxiously around – at John first, and then at each other – to see which of them had been shot. It turned out to be just a fire-cracker, thrown either by an idiot 'fan' or by one of the anti-Beatles protesters from the demo outside (a year and a half later, however, the gunshots were real as civil rights leader the Reverend Martin Luther King was shot dead in the city).

Three days after the Memphis gig, an undeterred Lennon stunned his Capitol 'handlers' by attacking US involvement in the Vietnam War at a New York press conference. 'We think of it every day, we don't like it. We think it's wrong.' John's comments were timely – the year had started with the US military resuming its bombing campaign against North Vietnam and June had seen a particularly heavy strike, against the northern capital Hanoi, which had left hundreds of civilians dead. There were grumblings about Lennon's remarks but the US press as a whole surprisingly failed to display serious outrage.

The next day The Beatles were at Shea Stadium where the crowd was down, from the previous year's 55,000 to a 'mere' 45,000. After more death threats The Beatles played their last-ever gig a few days later, behind six-foot-high iron cages at San Francisco's Candlestick Park, a venue some 4,000 miles from their English home town.

Not one of the first big rock festivals – at Monterey, Woodstock and Altamount – was to feature The Beatles, the band that made them all possible. John Lennon's Beatles, the biggest group in the world, could no longer play live anywhere in the US. It had, quite simply, become too dangerous.

It was almost certainly at this point, in August 1966, that the FBI and CIA files on John Lennon were started. For a major, internationally famous entertainer to speak out against the Vietnam War and for that act, at that time, not to have sparked official, if covert, action is almost inconceivable. A man who 'threatened' the political purity of America's youth was a man who threatened America's future.

We cannot know definitively, of course, as neither Lennon's CIA nor FBI files have ever been released in their entirety. The CIA, in particular, has a system that allows agents to start so-called '201 files' on the slightest pretext, files that rarely ever emerge into public scrutiny. Only four pages of Lennon's CIA file have ever been released, and these have only come to light because they were forwarded to – or in some cases sent from – the FBI.

The FBI's own Lennon files are also impossible to access in full. Despite the existence of America's Freedom of Information Act, it still took Professor Jon Wiener almost a decade of court action to get access to nearly 300 pages of John Lennon's FBI file – to this day many released sections, as well as ten whole documents, remain unseen on grounds of 'national security'…

On 25 June The Beatles performed Lennon's new song 'All You Need Is Love' live to a worldwide audience of over 400 million – the world's first truly global satellite link-up. Simplistic, sentimental and superficially straightforward, it still remains one of Lennon's finest songs, perhaps the first by any major pop artist that extols a poignantly universal love. The four-letter word 'love' no longer necessarily meant mum and dad or romantic hand-holding or a fast roll in the back of an automobile – in Lennon's composition it was the eternal, all-embracing everything, as much about brotherhood as Beethoven's Ninth Symphony. This is why we live and die and this is what we live and die for…

The track's unreal, semi-structured finale – complete with live orchestra and hand-clapping friends – represents one of popular music's most sublime moments. The dropping in of lines from 'She Loves You' and 'Yesterday' draws us in and yet adds emotional perspective – 'Can you see how far we've come in the three and a half years since we wrote these earlier, mere pop songs..?'

The Beatles' following album was the ground breaking *Sergeant Pepper's Lonely Hearts' Club Band*. The first, and in some ways still the best, rock concept album. Technically it was years ahead of its time, with producer George Martin using two synced up four-track recorders to create mixes that are difficult to beat even now.

Lyrically it saw the band both as third-person characters – years before Alice Cooper and David Bowie used such devices – and as future has-beens. Although much of *Pepper* came from McCartney it was Lennon who wrote its most dazzling track 'A Day In The Life' (all bar its 'alarm-clock middle eight'). 'A Day In The Life' starts with the bluesy tale of a millionaire's suicide, ends in orchestral cacophony and uses the drug catchphrase 'turn you on' (though it was McCartney – the nice, handsome Beatle – who would, within the year, be the first in the group to admit to taking LSD, a move some critics viewed as being an example of total, if misguided, honesty and others saw as being a crude 'street cred' attempt to wrestle control of the band from Lennon).

The year 1967 also saw the premiere of Dick Lester's blistering black comedy of British Army manners, *How I Won The War*, a superb yet surreal anti-war film that starred Michael Crawford and Lennon – the latter cast as the moaning reactionary Private Gripweed. Gripweed is fatally shot as the Army's North African cricket-pitch rolling team rolls victoriously into Nazi Germany. Lennon's part ends with him mortally wounded, telling the camera that he and the audience had both known all along that this was always going to happen, that he was always going to be shot and killed…

10 1968

'Hey hey LBJ! How many kids you killed today?'
– Demo chant

The year 1968 started off badly for the Johnson administration and rapidly got worse. On 19 January Japanese 'Vietniks' – anti-war students – stormed Tokyo's Foreign Ministry in protest against the visit of the USS *Enterprise*. Four days later the US Navy vessel *Pueblo* strayed too near the territorial waters of North Korea, an erratic Stalinist state that was still at war, technically at least, with one of America's biggest Asian allies, South Korea. North Korean sailors rapidly boarded and captured the USS *Pueblo* before it had barely had time to send a distress signal.

If LBJ was expecting a respite the next week he was in for an unpleasant surprise. On the night of 30–31 January, the Vietnamese 'Tet' New Year, the Vietcong NLF launched a massive wave of attacks deep inside South Vietnam. All the CIA and DIA lies about a weak, fading guerrilla force with 'falling morale' were blown apart as fighting actually broke out in Saigon, the southern capital, as well as in three dozen smaller towns.

America was stunned by pictures of dead US troops lying in their own blood within the very walls of the US Embassy, itself the scene of a fierce gun battle. The fact that the VC had used at least two suicide bombers – and that regular North Vietnamese soldiers had actually taken the ancient city of Hue after savage fighting – shocked both Johnson and the chiefs of staff. The short victorious war that Johnson had been promised was turning into a nightmare before his bloodshot eyes.

By 1 February, over 1,400 American troops had been killed or wounded. Still deep in denial, the US government proclaimed the Tet

Offensive a failure (though that didn't explain why over 10,000 more GIs were suddenly rushed to South Vietnam on emergency flights). Within two weeks the USAF was forced to bomb Saigon's own suburbs as VC insurgents struck again. Despite the setbacks, LBJ pronounced himself confident of winning the forthcoming election.

For almost a year, though, anti-war intellectual Allard Lowenstein had been single-handedly running an 'LBJ Must Go!' campaign. Because he gave lectures to the NSA he was labelled a CIA dupe by far-left student radicals. It didn't, however, deter him from insisting that someone from the Democratic Party must run against their own deeply compromised president.

It seemed like lunacy – no one from the same party had defeated an incumbent president in decades – but Lowenstein eventually flushed out an anti-war Democrat candidate in the shape of the clever but dour Eugene McCarthy (no relation to the Red-baiting Joe McCarthy). All the polls put McCarthy over 50 points behind LBJ but, as the impact of the Tet Offensive sank in – and as the US body bags came trickling home – the tide began to turn against Lyndon Baines Johnson (now more often known by his old college nickname of Lyndon 'Bullshit' Johnson).

On 7 March Bobby 'RFK' Kennedy gave the Senate a scorching speech demanding to know if the USA had the right to kill tens of thousands of people purely in the cause of a 'commitment to the South Vietnamese people? ...are we like the God of the Old Testament that we decide in Washington DC what cities, what towns, what hamlets are to be destroyed in Vietnam?'

A week later he announced that he would run for president and a few days later Eugene McCarthy made history by defeating LBJ in the Wisconsin primary.

In mid March in South Vietnam, at the My Lai 4 hamlet, soldiers of Charlie Company, 1st Battalion, 20th US infantry murdered over 450 unarmed men, women and children in a daylight orgy of rape and killing. Babies were bayoneted and shot before their stunned mothers were themselves sexually assaulted and shot. Laughing US troops kicked and punched children – the dead, the dying and the wounded – into mass graves before spraying them with bullets again.

At least two reporters and one photographer recorded the all-day massacre and one passing helicopter pilot – American Chief Warrant Officer Hugh C Thompson – was so enraged that he brought his craft down and managed to rescue ten children from the baying GIs – but Thompson only managed this after a furious row with Charlie Company's on-the-spot CO, one William L Calley Jr.

The US press ran stories *without* pictures later that week claiming the event had been a successful 'fire fight' with the Vietcong – US troops had apparently shown great bravery while killing over 120 armed VC insurgents. There was no mention of the murdered women and children, only more words about the fictional VC onslaught. No photos of the actual My Lai 4 massacre were to be printed for over a year and a half when the full story finally came out in 1970. There were other, less 'celebrated' mass killings of Vietnamese civilians by American forces – noticeably at My Akn and at Southang where 16 women and children were killed in a matter of seconds; two US marines were jailed for the latter slaughter – one for only five years – though their patrol leader Randy Herrod managed to get an acquittal after fellow marine Oliver North appeared as a character witness (no US troops were to spend years in jail over the bigger My Lai massacre since only Calley was charged and he was later released).

At the end of March 1968 Johnson decided he had suffered enough. He announced the suspension of US bombing against North Vietnamese forces north of the 20th parallel and concluded his speech with the words; 'I shall not seek and will not accept the nomination of my party for another term as president.'

The war in Vietnam had claimed the scalp of a second president. But, under the media spotlight, Eugene McCarthy had himself soon been revealed as a candidate with little charm and even less charisma. Still, at least he or RFK would make some serious attempt to end the slaughter in Southeast Asia.

But the Democratic Party's still ascendant right wing would not accept Eugene McCarthy or RFK, and VP Hubert Humphrey was swiftly drafted in on the 'peace with honour' ticket (that is, the continuation of the Vietnam War with frontline US troops).

Hubert Humphrey had most of the Democratic Party machinery behind him and it soon looked more and more like the only candidate with a chance of defeating Humphrey was Robert F Kennedy – who had the Kennedy glamour and the support of most liberals, blacks, Latinos and blue-collar workers.

On 4 April, the inspirational black civil rights leader Martin Luther King was shot dead in Memphis, Tennessee. He had gone to the Deep South city to support the garbage worker's strike – a multi-racial dispute.

King had embraced the anti-Vietnam War cause many months beforehand and had fought off attempts by Hoover's FBI to silence him. During the last speech of his life he'd spoken with eerie foresight of the promised land on earth and how he 'might not get there with you...'.

Within hours of the speech he was killed and riots erupted across the ghetto districts of America's cities. A thorough investigation of King's assassination was promised but that seemed to be undercut when officials stated, even before an arrest had been made, that there was definitely 'no conspiracy'.

In the end alleged racist James Earl Ray was arrested after taking a flight to England. The very fact that he'd flown the Atlantic seemed to prove his guilt to many Americans and his abrupt plea of guilty appeared to confirm this.

Yet a strange little FBI memo, to Hoover's 'friend' Clyde Tolson inadvertently hinted at something not being quite right:

'Now that Ray has been convicted and is serving a 99-year sentence, I would like to suggest that the Director allow us to choose a friendly capable author, or the Reader's Digest, and proceed with a book on the case...'.

Why did author have to be 'friendly'? The FBI isn't a pen pal organisation or dating agency. Why 'friendly'? What would an unfriendly one discover?

In the end George McMillan was presumably thought friendly enough and his *Making Of An Assassin* book sold thousands after being given a rave review by Jeremiah O'Leary; the latter was later revealed to be one of the 40 journalists – or 'agent-journalists' – who were actually on the CIA payroll.

Even with 'friendly' books, the actual case against Ray was not as watertight as it had at first seemed. As Ray changed his mind and began to proclaim his innocence, people began to ask about the Ray lookalike, complete with similar clothes and the same white Mustang car – right down to matching fender dents – seen in Memphis in the days leading up to King's assassination.

As with Lee Harvey Oswald, another man plagued by lookalikes, Ray even had an alias, Eric S Galt – and again here, there seemed to be two Eric Galts – one a shy, retiring character, the other a loud-mouthed racist drawing attention to himself.

In the seconds after the killing, one white Mustang went one way, bearing the killer, and a second appeared minutes later and went the other. A fake police-radio broadcast directed cars to chase one and not the other – almost certainly allowing the real killer to escape. No attempt seems to have been made by the Memphis police or the FBI to try and track down those behind the fake, and illegal, police broadcast.

And then there was the case of Marrell McCullough, the undercover Memphis policeman seen crouching over King's body just moments after the shooting. In 1997 it was revealed that McCullough had been a CIA agent since at least 1974. Loyd Jowers, in 1993, had admitted that he had been hired 25 years before to find a man to kill King – and the man he hired was not Ray.

When an ABC TV reporter later called the CIA and asked to speak to McCullough, the latter admitted that he did know Jowers. When told the call was about the MLK assassination McCullough slammed the phone down. McCullough today denies being MLK's assassin and says he did not join the CIA until after the killing.

Jailed killer Jules Ricco Kimble – who in 1963 had a PO box in the same New Orleans building as JFK assassination suspects Oswald and Ferrie – once boasted of his involvement in the King murder, saying that Ray was involved too, but only as an unwitting fall-guy.

After making their own extensive inquiries, Martin Luther King's family joined in the campaign for a re-trial of James Earl Ray. They no longer believed Ray was guilty of killing their most famous family member. Unfortunately, Ray died before a re-trial was permitted.

After releasing the 'Lady Madonna' single and decamping from the Maharishi's Indian base, Lennon and McCartney appeared on America's NBC *Tonight* show – partly to explain the concept behind their latest venture, Apple Corps. Before the interview was through Lennon raised eyebrows by telling host Joe Garagiola that continuing US involvement in the Vietnam War was 'insanity'. The solution to American political injustice was, Lennon continued, 'to change the establishment', a comment later echoed by various counter-cultural gurus ('Don't hate the media, *become* the media!').

A week later Lennon changed his own establishment – after 18 months of flirting with avant-garde Japanese artist Yoko Ono he finally invited her to his Weybridge home (wife Cynthia was away at the time).

'I played her all the tapes that I'd made,' Lennon later said, 'some comedy and stuff and some electronic stuff. She was suitably impressed and said, "Let's make one ourselves!" So we made *Two Virgins*, it was midnight when we started and dawn when we finished and then we made love at dawn. It was very beautiful.'

Two months after King's assassination, young America's last hope, Robert Kennedy, was shot dead. He died at LA's Ambassador Hotel, within minutes of hearing he'd won the Californian primary. His murder, so soon after King's, stunned a blood-soaked America.

His alleged killer was Sirhan Sirhan, who fired a handgun eight times from between two and six feet away from Kennedy. As there were dozens of witnesses Sirhan was soon bundled away and charged with the murder. As far as the LAPD was concerned it was case closed – Sirhan wasn't crazy (despite the later 'lone nut' stories) and he was seen in the act. And he was alone.

But the LAPD's story – and that of its SUS (Special Unit Senator) investigators didn't hold up, despite the support of the FBI.

For a start there were too many bullets, RFK was hit three times and a fourth shot ripped his clothes, at least five other people took bullets and there were two more in the door frames. That total, of 11, is three more than Sirhan's gun could possibly hold (there were also those witnesses who felt that Sirhan's shots didn't actually sound like real bullets, more like a cap gun or starting pistol).

Then there was the fact that the official coroner, Dr Thomas Noguchi, later revealed: the fatal shot had been fired into RFK's ear from *behind*, from less than two inches away. Effectively at point blank. And yet Sirhan had been between two feet and six feet away, in front of Kennedy.

Sirhan himself behaved curiously – he'd gone on firing his gun even while being beaten by six people, receiving extensive bruising to his eye, a badly sprained ankle and smashed finger. Such a beating would fell an ox, yet the slight Sirhan kept plugging away, his eyes 'beautifully peaceful' according to witnesses. He seemed to other witnesses to be in a trance.

Afterwards, in custody, despite the summer heat, he had the chills – something he was to repeat after hypnosis sessions with Dr Diamond in prison. When asked why he'd killed RFK Sirhan didn't seem to know – though, after discussions with his defence attorney, he later claimed it was to support Arab nationalism after Kennedy had supported the sale of US jets to Israel (but RFK hadn't made public his jets to Israel statement until days *after* Sirhan had filled his dairies with endless scribbles: 'RFK Must Die! RFK Must Die! RFK Must Die Before June 5th!').

The police and FBI ignored all this, ignored those who'd seen a security guard with a drawn gun and ignored the other accomplices seen with Sirhan on the night (and at previous RFK meetings and later at a rifle range). When the press picked up on the girl with the polka-dot dress – later found to be an Iranian whose father was linked to American intelligence – the LAPD response was to browbeat the two main 'polka-dot' witnesses into withdrawing their testimony (they and others had seen the 'polka-dot girl' running away with a young man, the girl happily shouting that, 'We've shot Kennedy!').

Sirhan's bullets were more problematic. The SUS/FBI answers were simple – it was decided that, of Sirhan's eight bullets, three of them were 'magic bullets' that had bounced round all over the place, nipping in and out of walls and causing exactly the right amount of injuries and damage (the two bullets in the door frames had, by now, disappeared since the LAPD had had the frames ripped out and destroyed, a strange way to treat forensic evidence).

All this manipulation of evidence still left the problem of the firing distances. Sirhan's gun being at least two feet away in front – and perhaps six feet away in front – and the fatal bullet coming in from less than two inches from behind. Again the official response was basic but effective – the RFK autopsy report was simply withheld from the defence team until the trial had already started. A confused Sirhan later pleaded guilty anyway and the case was, for the moment, uneasily closed.

Many researchers, however, believed that the real killer must have been one or more of the security guards. There were no police present at the time of the shooting, only security guards. And only the security guards were armed, only they were close enough, only they were right behind RFK at the time of the shooting...

On the other side of the Atlantic in 1968, Labour leader Harold Wilson found himself increasingly under fire from critics on the right. Under Wilson, Labour had done away with the death sentence, and had legalised abortion and homosexuality for adults over 21. They'd also passed the Race Relations Act, outlawing race discrimination, and increased the pressure on both of Africa's biggest 'racist' states, South Africa and Rhodesia. To add insult to injury Wilson had refused to send British troops to fight alongside the Americans in Vietnam, even though a fellow Commonwealth country, Australia, had already done so.

Late in the year there were at least two secret meetings attended by several BBC governors, British Army chiefs, and members of MI5 and MI6. Such was the establishment's panic that the possibility of an anti-Labour coup was seriously discussed – a piece of paranoid treason no doubt prompted by the less-than-rational belief of many CIA high-ups that Britain's prime minister was really a Russian spy.

At the same time musician Mick Farren and his rock band The Pink Fairies were stopped twice on England's M1 motorway. Farren and co were astonished to find that the cops weren't interested in drugs, they were actually looking for guns...

Musically, the '60s ended in Britain for the Lennons with a series of gigs by the Plastic Ono Band (the latter being John and Yoko plus whatever other musicians happened to be around). The chosen venue was the large Lyceum Theatre, round the corner from the East End of London's The Strand, in the West End. The Lyceum then was a magical place to see gigs, often it would stay open until four or five in morning – virtually the only thousand-seater in London to do so – before the ageing, sliding roof would grind open. Young Londoners would then glimpse the stars above before the dawn bleached them out. Though, like the other concert halls, it stopped serving alcohol well before midnight, the Lyceum was still an amazing place for a teenager to visit in its 1968–74 heyday.

The Lyceum was amazing too during the Plastic Ono Band gigs, with Lennon saturating the Vic-wardian hall with feedback and wild, driving rock. Throw in Yoko's wailing vocals and some of the best guitarists in England and you had a night, or three, to remember. Lennon himself regarded the Lyceum gigs as being influential, the first real 'heavy rock' nights in Britain, and in all the most important senses – volume, spectacle and attitude – he was probably right (young punks Glen Matlock and the late Joe Strummer are both said to have been teenage visitors to the Lyceum in this period, several years before they kick-started The Sex Pistols and The Clash – although Matlock, now a successful solo artist who still tours with the reformed Pistols, was a heavy drinker for years and has no definite memory of seeing the Plastic Ono Band at the Lyceum, a venue the Pistols themselves were to play in 1976).

11 Concert Security

'Source advised police officers patrolled only on the outside'
— *FBI memo, December 1971*

Airtel   **4/23/70**
To: Special Agents in Charge (SACS), New York, Los Angeles.
From: Director, FBI/
JOHN LENNON [next words blanked out]
GEORGE HARRISON [next words blanked out]
PATRICIA HARRISON [next words blanked out]
INFORMATION CONCERNING [next words blanked out]

On 4/22/70 a representative of the Department of State advised
that the American Embassy in London had submitted
information showing the captioned individuals planned to
depart from London, England on 4/23/70 via TWA Flight 761
which will arrive in Los Angeles at 7.15 local time. These
individuals are affiliated with The Beatles musical group and
Lennon will be travelling under the name Chambers while the
Harrisons are using the name Masters.

Lennon and the Harrisons will remain in Los Angeles until
5/6/70 for business discussions with Capitol Records and other
enterprises. They will travel to New York City on 5/7/70 for
further business discussions and will return to London on or
about 5/16/70.

Waivers were granted by the Immigration and Naturalization Service (INS) and the Embassy was to issue visas on 4/22/70.
In this case waivers were necessary in view of the ineligibility

Lennon meets the press, July 1966. The Beatles' tour of the Far East had just ended with Filipino officials attacking the billion-selling band

August 1966. Young anti-Beatle protestors in Jackson, Mississippi, burn Beatles' records, angered by Lennon's 'bigger than Jesus' remark

Leaving a London court, October 1968. The detective who 'found' John's cannabis is later convicted of 'perverting the course of justice'

Just months before the Lennons revive his campaign, the father of James Hanratty – executed for 1961's A6 murder – protests alone in Westminster

The most public honeymoon ever. May 1969 sees the Lennons continuing their Bed Peace gesture in Toronto

'Laugh bag' smiles in Montreal, December 1969. The Lennons went on to meet Canada's Premier, Pierre Trudeau, just before ITV declared Lennon, JFK and Chairman Mao the 'Men Of The Decade'

Nixon with Elvis at the White House, December 1970. Presley attacked The Beatles' 'anti-American' spirit

Dressed in uniform, a deadpan ex-Beatle and his wife protest against the Vietnam War in 1971

John enters NYC's INS offices in May 1972, as FBI memos prompt the INS to demand mental examinations of him and Yoko

Lennon with May Pang during a 'lost weekend' that lasted 15 months and saw his first solo chart-toppers

Mark David Chapman, just back from Beirut, with co-worker Mary Webster at the Fort Chaffe Vietnamese refugee camp, Arkansas, 1975

The Lennons in late 1980: cool together, but John's assassination is just days away

John with young Sean. This was Lennon's parental second chance: he wanted to avoid the long absences he'd inflicted on first son, Julian

Chapman leaving a New York police station, December 1980. The NYPD had already claimed that Chapman was 'deranged'

A week after John's death, fans gathered in Central Park for a vigil which was observed by millions worldwide. On the same day, the Assassination Info Committee claimed Lennon's killing was 'political'

The plaque at the Apple building, Baker Street, unveiled by Sir John Mills in April 2003

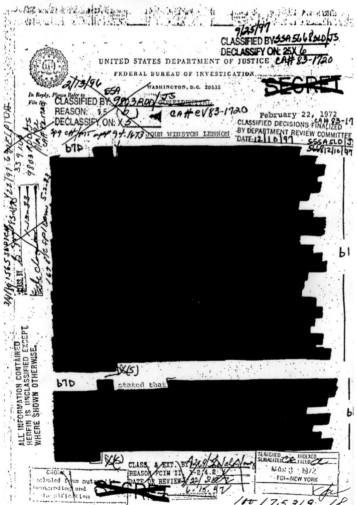

An extract from the released FBI files. A large number of pages are completely blanked out, more than half at the request of the British government

of these three individuals to enter the US due to their reputations in England as narcotic users.
[next words blanked out]

Airtel to New York
Re: John Lennon, George Harrison, Patricia Harrison.

While Lennon and the Harrisons have shown no propensity to become involved in violent antiwar demonstrations, each recipient remain alert for any information of such activity on their part or for information indicating they are using narcotics. Submit any pertinent information obtained in form suitable for dissemination...

On 23 April 1970 John Lennon, Yoko Ono, George Harrison and Harrison's wife Patti Boyd had indeed flown from London to Los Angeles. Although J Edgar Hoover's above 'Airtel' – an internal FBI message that must be sent the day it's written – doesn't mention Yoko Ono, the trip was mainly her idea, so that Lennon, now her third husband, could undergo primal therapy at Arthur Janov's Primal Institute in LA.

The couple had been married in March 1969, enjoying the most public honeymoon in history by inviting the world press to a series of 'Bed-Ins for Peace' in Amsterdam and Vienna. Middle-aged journalists present at these events were angry, in some cases to the point of apoplexy, accusing the Lennons of 'cynically exploiting' their fame for peace (many of the disappointed reporters had expected the 'bed-ins' to feature sex, or least some nudity).

Later in the year the Lennons had also met the parents of James Hanratty, the burglar who'd been hanged – many believe wrongly – for the 1961 A6 murder. The Lennons listened sympathetically to the Hanrattys' story and later gave them money for a film to fund the re-opening of the case.

There had, of course, been previous American complaints about John and Yoko's 1968 album *Two Virgins* for, under the sleeve's brown paper wrapper, the couple had appeared nude on the cover. There were even nine pages in Lennon's FBI files concerning it, though four of these were letters from congressmen – all along the lines of 'must we fling this filth at our pop kids?' – and most of the rest were about a student demo at the University of Hartford, Connecticut (the students were complaining about the suspension of the campus newspaper over an editorial decision to run the *Two Virgins'* sleeve).

But the April 1970 Airtel from the FBI's boss was the first time, officially, the Bureau had begun to generate its own paperwork on John Ono Lennon.

By then, in 1970, John Lennon was hardly alone in his anti-war stance – protestors half a million strong had marched against the Vietnam War the year before. And even the Airtel admits that neither Lennon nor the Harrisons had shown any 'propensity to become involved in violent antiwar demonstrations'.

Lennon – like the Harrisons – was a British-born subject. He was also, at that point, a British-based subject who was merely visiting the United States for a few days. A strange subject for the domestic wing of America intelligence to be interested in. Why were the LA and NYC FBI offices alerted? In case of the unlikely event of Lennon inviting arrest and imprisonment by taking drugs publicly? (It would have to be public since there is, after all, no mention of surveillance – electronic, telephonic or otherwise.)

Or were these field offices contacted in case The Beatles' founder suddenly reversed the philosophy of a lifetime, ignored his 'non-violent propensity' and physically attacked a police officer at a peace demo...?

Despite this being a Freedom of Information Act (FOIA) release – issued over 18 years after it was sent and some 16 years after Hoover's death – there are still a few words that FBI staffers have blanked out. What are these, the names of informers? Just who was it amongst the US Embassy's Department of State workers – or Britain's showbiz establishment – that was keeping tabs on Lennon before he'd even left England? And why?

The very next day – 24 April 1970 – brought Hoover a couriered Airtel from Ottawa, Canada, that later resulted in an FBI 'triumph'. The message, from the FBI's Ottawa Legat concerned a 'PEACE STATION

NETWORK, IS – MISCELLANEOUS (NEW LEFT – FOREIGN INFLUENCE – CANADA).'

After 1969's successful Toronto Peace Festival – featuring John and Yoko, Eric Clapton, Chuck Berry and Bo Diddley – the Lennons had suggested setting up a 'loose organisation' of radio stations promoting both peace and the 3–5 July 1970 Mosport Peace Festival. A 'youth-orientated' event at which the Lennons and others would again play live.

Ritchie Yorke and John Brower had taken it upon themselves to coordinate and promote the festival, and their Toronto-based Peace Station Network (PSN) had approached a Canadian radio station, WJWL.

After refusing to air a five-minute PSN peace programme, the station's conservative manager Edward Marzoa was lobbied by a local youth delegation determined to hear what they had been missing. Marzoa agreed to at least listen to the programme before making a final decision but he contacted the Royal Canadian Mounted Police on 18 March as he suspected the subversive worst about the young people behind PSN:

'(...I would like to know who their officers are; what their purposes are; how they are financed; and why the Canadian base. I have my suspicions... The [airtime] decision is of course mine, I would appreciate however, something more concrete than my intuition to support whatever that decision may be...)'

On 21 April the RCMP's Superintendent Chisholm acknowledged receipt of Marzoa's letter concerning the '5-minute "peace" programs' but regretted that the RCMP was:

'unable to supply you with the information which you requested as government policy requires us to liaise with the Federal Bureau of Investigation in matters related to enquiries of this nature. We therefore suggest you redirect your enquiry to the Federal Bureau of Investigation.'

It's an astonishing reply really; a police officer of the sovereign state of Canada telling one of the nation's subjects to write to the foreign Federal

Bureau of Investigation about a Canadian-based radio network – before the same letters are anyway secretly forwarded to the FBI.

Was Chisholm aware of an FBI file on PSN? Or was Lennon's FBI file – barely ten pages at this point and, officially at least, virtually dormant – actually far larger and already highly active? Had Chisholm already been told to send any Lennon-related material to Hoover's FBI?

Whatever the answer to the latter question, the FBI eventually got what it wanted from its Canadian correspondence. The Mosport location for the peace festival was vetoed by Ontario's Municipal Board while the PSN got very few Canadian radio broadcasts and Lennon never again played north of the border.

In December 1970, Lennon's one-time hero Elvis Presley met President Nixon at the White House. The meeting was about Presley wanting to 'reach' the kids who were drifting into drugs. The man who's hip-swivelling stage act had sold rock 'n' roll to the world now wanted 'to restore some respect for the flag which was being lost'.

Nixon listened attentively as Presley explained that part of the problem was The Beatles, who 'had been a real force for anti-American spirit...they had come to this country, made their money and then returned to England'.

Nixon nodded in agreement, then indicated that he felt that those taking drugs were also in the vanguard of the anti-American protests (funny how being against the Vietnam War seemed, in Nixon's mind, to automatically make someone 'anti-American', it was as if, mentally, he was still on McCarthy's witchunt against 'Un-Americans').

Presley, after a few more expressions of loyalty, then asked the President to meet a couple of his 'Graceland mafia' cronies. Nixon agreed and after a few moments with the hangers-on, both they and Elvis were on their way out of the White House. It was Nixon, not the slightest bit over-awed, who warned Elvis about losing his street credibility. Presley himself – depressed, pilled-up and with his marriage going wrong – was too busy trying to save America from Lennon's Beatles to worry about damaging his own fading career...

Neither Presley nor Nixon bothered to mention the biggest news story of the moment – the mass bombing of North Vietnam, US bombing which had recently resumed after a two-year break, killing thousands of civilians. One bombing wave was so severe it left a school of hundreds permanently deafened.

In London, one Beatle was about to drop his own bombshell – on 30 December Paul McCartney launched a High Court suit to end The Beatles' business partnership...

One year later, on 11 December 1971, and Lennon's official FBI file ground into life again. Two months after issuing his second solo album – *Imagine* with its classic universal brotherhood title track that some took to be 'communistic' – the former Beatle had performed live at the John Sinclair Freedom Rally at the Crisler Arena in Ann Arbor, Michigan, on 10 December.

Lennon's first live US gig in five years was a benefit played with Yoko – and preceded by Stevie Wonder, Bob Seger, Commander Cody, David Peel and Phil Ochs – before an audience of some 15,000. Lennon wound the event up – after speeches by the likes of Allen Ginsberg and 'Yippie leader' Jerry Rubin – with songs like the freshly penned 'John Sinclair' (though the lyrics to this soon appeared among the sleeve notes of Lennon's forthcoming *Sometime In New York City*, the FBI deemed them 'confidential' and withheld the document in question for years).

A few weeks before the rally, John Sinclair had been sentenced to a staggering ten years in jail for the heinous crime of selling two joints to an undercover police officer.

Sinclair was a former White Panther, one of the foul-mouthed Yippie-type radicals. One of his less offensive '60s statements read: 'F— your woman till she can't stand up! Our program of rock, dope and f—ing in the streets is a program of total freedom for everyone!'

Though, to give him his due, Sinclair had helped disrupt Mayor Daley's grotesque Democratic National Convention of 1968 (when radicals, young Democrats and even passers-by were beaten and gassed by the Chicago police).

And it was because of the forthcoming Republican National Convention (RNC) that the FBI was watching Lennon. At the RNC President Nixon's pro-war stance was to be rubber-stamped as he was to be renominated to lead the Republican party into the November 1972

US election. The Bureau was convinced the Ann Arbor benefit was merely a taste of things to come, a forerunner of a nationwide radical rock tour that would culminate at the RNC in San Diego in August.

The speeches at Ann Arbor – secretly recorded and then transcribed word for word by the FBI g-men – certainly showed hostility both towards Nixon, his drugs policy and the status quo he represented.

Radical lawyer William Kunstler was busy on another case and so sent a tape to broadcast through the PA – a tape that was then, of course, taped in turn by the FBI. He began by talking about Sinclair's imprisonment.

'...JOHN is in jail for two essential reasons; first of all he is a political person who calls into question the validity of the superstate which seeks to control all of us and destroys those it cannot readily dominate. Secondly, his harsh sentence dramatizes the absurdity of our marijuana laws which are irrational, unjust and indefensible. Recently the National Institute of Mental Health submitted to the Congress its 176-page report "Marijuana and Health", which comes to the conclusion that, quote, For the bulk of smokers, marijuana does not seem to be harmful, end quote. Yet it is made a crime in every state with penalties ranging in severity from life to six months in jail. On the other hand, conventional cigarettes can be legally sold as long as they bear a legend on the package that they can cause serious illness or death...'

Another, unnamed speaker, who may be Jerry Rubin or MC Bob Rudnick, cranks the political rhetoric up a notch:

'...it's the only way we are going to attack capitalism. To expropriate from that capitalistic system the goods, the techno-logy etc, to put it down in the poor oppressed communities, all of us, the people that are oppressed and us too and everybody processing it and giving it away free. It's the only way I know [to] start attacking the monster of capitalism. A monster of charging people money for everything they get, we're saying the music is free, the life is free, the world is free and if it ain't free, let's start getting our chains off now. The psychology chains and the chains of oppression...

...if we don't have the chains off of us they are going to annihilate us. They are going to annihilate us by polluting this earth, the capitalists and fascists they are going to do this here. We [are] saying the universe belongs to the people, Mars belongs to the people, and the people belong to the people, all power to the people. Thank you very much, Right on, Power to the people.'

Rubin, surprisingly articulate, then raged against the president and all his works while speaking about the Lennons as the previous speaker had – before, one suspects, it had actually been confirmed that they had turned up.

'...it's really incredible that JOHN and YOKO are gonna be here tonight, and [we] should really think of what that meaning is. Cause it's really a committed act by people who are very involved in music, who are identifying to the culture you and I are part of. The family you and I are part of and for them to come on this stage, and for JOHN and YOKO to sing a song about the IRA and Attica State, It's really incredible. It shows that right now we can really build the movement all across the country [applause]...

It's like a whole cultural renaissance is about to begin and if JOHN and YOKO can come here we really have to go back to high school and college and communities and rebuild the movement, to rebuild the revolution because all the people who say the movement and revolution is over should see what's going on right here, because it doesn't look over to me.

But there are, there are a lot of problems, for example the amount of heroin and dope that is smoked in the black and white youth communities... heroin is poison and you know it get its source from Southeast Asia, Laos and then it's shipped by the CIA back to the US as a poison to poison us so we don't make a revolution, that's why they are pushing all this heroin into us [applause]...

...we want JOHN SINCLAIR out of prison, we want him out of prison to help us organize the music at San Diego [applause]...

...NIXON's program is not for winding down the war but for winding down the anti-war movement, it's the most cynical appeal to us, to say it doesn't matter that more people are being killed today than there were last month, it doesn't matter that there are more people killed last month than there were under JOHNSON, as long as they are Asians, as long as they are not Americans...

...Now one last point, I also came to hear JOHN and YOKO sing a song to the liberation of JOHN SINCLAIR and the other prisoners. We have the power, we have the strength if, like the Vietnamese and the Cambodian and the Laotians, we do not allow the government, visible or invisible, to pacify us, if we do not allow them to convince [us] that we are weak and impotent and nothing we do will matter. Ever since 1964, the press, the dove press, mind you, and the government has been saying the war is ending and the anti-war movement is dead, but it has never been through, and it is not through today, the war will not go away by itself, and JOHN SINCLAIR will not get free by [himself]...'

Despite ending in rousing applause the event was slated by *Detroit News* reporter Bill Gray – a Bill billed that day as 'News Amusement Writer'. While admitting it was the Lennon name that bought most of the 15,000 listeners to the Crisler Arena, Gray attacked Yoko for her inability to stay on key before finding Lennon's contribution, of three new songs, similarly disappointing. The new material was not up to the former Beatles' 'usual standards' and Gray found him insufficiently star-like, a man who was flippantly playing the working-class hero.

Though he didn't play the demanding diva, thus failing to placate the local press, Lennon did go down well singing 'John Sinclair' – reading the lyrics off papers taped to the mic stand. He didn't, in the end, sing any songs dedicated to the IRA (he was, however, sympathetic to the Irish Republican cause, at least until the wave of bombings that shook Northern Ireland and mainland Britain between the summers of 1972 and 1975).

Such sympathies, like some sections of the above speeches, are easy to condemn with 20/20 hindsight. But some of what was said that night still rings true – and much of the passion, the hope and the lingering innocence of the '60s were shown to be still alive and kicking as the tape reels of the 'invisible government' turned.

And Rubin was right in one sense for, messy and over the top though much of that night was, it was something new for a world-famous rock star to be standing on a stage alongside barefoot radicals, demanding an end to both war and the harsh imprisonment of those who were merely being a little reckless with their own health...

The initials SM and IS appear on these particular FBI documents – SM standing for Security Matters and IS for Internal Security (the leading captions are 'SM – New Left' and 'IS – White Panther Party'). The first informer, or source, has his – or her – name blanked out while the second is identified as the 'Intelligence Unit of the Michigan State Police'.

Seven different FBI field offices received between two and five copies of this nine-page document – along with the 'WFO', another blanked-out recipient and the National Student Association. The latter was supposedly independent but was actually a CIA-supported nationwide organisation.

So, at least 17 copies were sent out initially – plus those Letter Head Memo (LHM) copies that, like all of Lennon's FBI LHMs went out to the CIA, the Secret Service, US Army Intelligence, US Naval Intelligence, the State Department and the INS. Much of this document was withheld after its initial FOIA release. Confusion also reigns over the page numbering – page two is crossed out and numbered as three, page three is crossed out and numbered as four, and so on. Page nine is missing in its entirety. Possibly by accident, probably by design.

More disturbingly still, one of the half pages that was withheld for a dozen years shows a strange fascination with the event's – and therefore Lennon's – security.

'Source advised 10 off-duty Ann Arbor police officers patrolled the area near the rally hall.

Source advised the services of the off-duty police officers were obtained and paid for at a cost of $150.00 by the WPP at Ann Arbor, Michigan. Source advised police officers patrolled only on the outside of the rally hall and were not permitted to enter the rally.

Source advised the entire portion of the rally hall was patrolled by so-called WP Rangers...'

Why are these matters of such import to the informants? The informants presumably being in this case the officers of Michigan State's Intelligence Unit who had dutifully noted down all of the above details.

Why was the recording of these details hidden by the FBI for as long as was legally possible? Is it just another long-hidden FBI red herring, like the careful hiding of the long public 'John Sinclair' lyrics? Or something more?

Were these security matters important because, at some point, the FBI or CIA – or paid troublemakers – were aiming to violently disrupt such events and thus needed to know how the organisers would police?

Or did it go beyond disruption? Into an area that's far more deadly? It was a security guard who many later came to regard as the real assassin of Robert Kennedy just three years before.

The fact that few more such concerts took place – and no major ones reached the 1972 RNC – is neither here nor there. No one in the US intelligence community could possibly have foreseen that at the time. And the systematic mugging, kidnapping and deporting of peace demonstrators at the RNC was seriously suggested a few months later to Nixon's Attorney General John Mitchell.

This incredibly irresponsible idea came from Nixon troubleshooter Gordon Liddy and his ex-CIA agent associate E Howard Hunt, a man with his fingers in many pies. Hunt was a close friend of both Richard Helms and Allen Dulles, the former being CIA deputy director until 1965, director until 1973 and US Ambassador to Iran from1973–76 (Helms was also the creator of the CIA's MK/ULTRA mind-control project and its Southeast Asian assassination programme) while Dulles – brother of John Foster Dulles – was CIA director until sacked by President John F Kennedy in the aftermath of the 1961 Cuban Bay of Pigs fiasco.

Dulles later served on the Warren Commission – alongside Earl Warren and Republican politician Gerald Ford – supposedly investigating JFK's assassination with rigour. Hunt himself had been the political officer for the Bay of Pigs operation, a failed invasion that was planned, in part, by Richard Nixon during the dying months of the 1952–60 Eisenhower administration when he (Nixon) was still vice-president. Hunt is also alleged to have forged cables falsely blaming Kennedy for ordering the killing of South Vietnamese President Diem.

In the end, Nixon's Attorney General Mitchell rejected Hunt and Liddy's first plan too. Mugging and hijacking protesters at the 1972 RNC just wasn't on – it wasn't the illegality that worried America's senior law-enforcement official, it was just the excessive financial cost.

But Mitchell did agree to listen to Liddy and Hunt's alternative suggestion. The latter was another criminal action, a plan to break into the Democratic Party HQ in Washington DC's Watergate complex, there to photograph documents and plant listening devices.

12 Insanity (April–May 1972)

'We've got to get Nixon out, we've got to stop the automated war in Vietnam. It's power if we vote together...we ought to go to both Conventions...and, not violently, make our presence felt. If we do anything any other way, we'll be killed.'

– Jerry Rubin, 1972

Christmas 1971 had seen the Lennons repeat their 'Happy Xmas! War Is Over (if you want it)' poster campaign, though they still didn't have a finished record to go with it. It pioneered the now huge overlap between concept art, music media and advertising (the difference between these independent works and the much-sponsored efforts of today's concept artists is similarly huge – the Lennons were, after all, first, they were also trying to save Vietnam's peasantry from extermination, a higher aim, one would have thought, than the petty greed that motivates most of today's Saatchi groupies...).

Perhaps because of this campaign, 12 January 1972 saw one of the more threatening FBI Lennon documents brought into play. A Special Agent – name deleted – reported the fairly banal fact the John and Yoko had appeared with Jerry Rubin at a press conference shown on citywide New York television channel WABC-TV.

After noting that only Lennon himself had been interviewed by the TV reporter present – and that 'Rubin appeared to have his hair cut much shorter than previously shown in other photographs' – the SA had hand-written in huge, underlined capitals, '<u>ALL EXTREMISTS SHOULD BE CONSIDERED DANGEROUS</u>'.

Remembering that this is being written about 'peacenik' John Lennon makes it seem that much more startling. And ominous.

On 25 April 1972 an FBI agent sent a confidential teletype to the 'Honourable HR Haldeman, Assistant to the President, The White House, Washington DC'.

The document stated that John Winston Lennon – 'a British citizen and a former member of The Beatles singing group' – had been convicted in London of 'possession of dangerous drugs'. These 'dangerous drugs' consisted of around 200 'grains' of hash that were allegedly found in Ringo Starr's Montagu Square flat when Lennon and Yoko had replaced Jimi Hendrix as temporary tenants there in October 1968.

Lennon always denied the hash was his, saying he had 'cleaned the place up' after the *Daily Mirror* reporter Don Short had told him the previous month that Detective Sergeant Pilcher and certain other officers in the Drugs Squad 'were after Lennon'. Although believing that the cannabis had been planted, Lennon still entered a guilty plea and paid the £150 fine – £3,000 in today's money – to prevent the fuss a 'not guilty' plea might have caused, a fuss that could have led to Yoko Ono's deportation from the UK (such a 'crime' today would not even lead to an arrest in most parts of the UK, Holland and northern Germany – and on 8 November 1972 Detective Sergeant Pilcher was himself charged, in a London court, with conspiracy 'to pervert the course of justice').

Despite this heinous outrage and his 'apparent ineligibility' Lennon had, the agent noted, somehow obtained a US visa in 1971 and entered the States. The agent then informed Nixon's assistant that during

'February 1972, a confidential source who has furnished reliable information in the past, advised that Lennon had contributed $75,000 to a newly organized New Left group formed to disrupt the Republican National Convention [RNC].

The visas of Lennon and his wife Yoko Ono expired on 29 February 1972 and since that time Immigration and Naturalization Service (INS) have been attempting to deport them...their attorney stated that Lennon felt he was being deported due to his outspoken remarks concerning US policy in Southeast Asia...the attorney requested a delay...then read into the court record that Lennon had been appointed to the

President's Council for Drug Abuse (Nat. Comm. on Marijuana and Drug Abuse) and to the faculty of New York University NYC...a second confidential source who has furnished reliable information in the past, advised that Lennon continues to be a heavy user of narcotics. On 21 April 1972, a third confidential source....advised that there was no information available indicating that Lennon had been appointed to the National Commission on Marijuana and Drug Abuse...'

Although this teletype didn't classify Lennon under 'Security Matters – Revolutionary Activities' as previous FBI memos had – and although it conceded that New York University had indeed offered Lennon a temporary teaching post of sorts – it still ended on a chilling note...'this information is also being furnished to the Acting Attorney General. Pertinent information concerning Lennon is being furnished to the Department of State and INS on a regular basis.'

It was criminal really – there were Nazis, child-molesters and heroin dealers that had been given American green cards – the right to stay in the US – and now the Lennons were being denied one purely on the basis of a single, suspicious cannabis bust (the green card denial was even more outrageous in Yoko's case, she had no criminal convictions at all – apparently just being a friend or relative of John Lennon was enough to get one blacklisted in 1972).

Four days earlier, FBI agent RL Shackelford informed bureau superior ES Miller that 'New York City Police Department currently [is] attempting to develop enough information to arrest both Lennons for narcotic use...'.

Despite this hoped-for arrest there was, however, 'a real possibility that the subject will not be deported from the US in the near future'. Shackelford then baldly stated that 'subject's activities [are] being closely followed and any information developed indicating violation of Federal laws will be immediately furnished to pertinent agencies in [an] effort to neutralize any disruptive activities of subject. Information developed to date has been furnished...to INS and State Department...also been furnished Internal Security Division of the Department.'

In other words, the FBI, the State Department and the SD's own Internal Security Division were all trying to lean on the immigration service in an attempt to get the Lennons deported. Republican Senator Strom Thurmond had already written to the attorney general complaining about Lennon's presence (the letter had the scrawled footnote 'can we keep him out?').

The next day, 22 April, John and Yoko defiantly joined the National Peace Rally in New York protesting against the USA's increased carpet bombing of North Vietnam – both of them addressed the 20,000 strong crowd...as well as the FBI agents who were also present.

The couple had initially flown to New York to try to find, and win custody of, Yoko's eight-year-old daughter Kyoko. In December 1971, in Houston, Texas, they'd come close to achieving that goal and Ono's ex, Anthony Cox, had even been jailed for five days for refusing to let her see her child. In March 1972 Yoko finally won the case, legally at least, and a Houston court awarded her custody of Kyoko.

But Cox grabbed the child and disappeared into the night. The search for them continued, fruitlessly at first. John and Yoko had previously spent thousands chasing Cox halfway across the world, via Spain and Trinidad, but the sincerity of even this maternal quest was to be questioned after the Lennons had dared attend the National Peace Rally...

On 1 May, John and Yoko appeared in New York City court to try and obtain an injunction against the INS proceedings. INS representative Vincent A Schiano told the court that John's UK drugs conviction was 'not likely to be overturned' and though Schiano admitted that there had been a large volume of mail opposing the Lennons' deportation, he also claimed that there was a similar amount of correspondence supporting the action.

Lennon's lawyer Leon Wildes read a letter from Mayor John Lindsay publicly requesting that the INS proceedings be dropped as the couple in question were 'distinguished artists in the music field and are an asset to us', they were only being treated this way by the INS because they were 'outspoken' on the 'major issues of the day'.

The court made no decision beyond postponing the hearing until 9 May. This postponement was itself postponed to 17 May. By that time

Lennon had appeared on Dick Cavett's TV show and told the stunned audience that he and his lawyer's phones were being tapped, that he himself was being followed by government agents. Lennon spoke out after hearing clicks, feedback and conversation fragments – the usual evidence of pre-digital phone tapping.

'Guys would always be standing on the street opposite. If I got in a car they'd get in cars and follow me, blatantly. They wanted me to know I was being followed.'

Photographer Bob Gruen, a close friend of Lennon's, had also noticed. 'I was taking pictures of John in a recording studio one day and after I'd left I noticed this car tailing me for miles, right into town. I was a little freaked and so I called John. He said, "yeah, they've been following me for weeks".'

But, as Lennon knew, the media sometimes has a little power of its own. 'The day after the [Dick Cavett] TV show, there was nobody standing outside.'

The night before the hearings of 17 May, the FBI's NYC office once again wired its Acting Director – the temporary replacement for the recently deceased J Edgar Hoover – on the subject of 'John Winston Lennon'. The teletype revealed that Schiano had told the FBI he was going to use three key arguments in his battle to evict John and Yoko Lennon from US soil.

Firstly, he was going to allege that the Lennons' 'claim' that Anthony Cox had abducted Yoko's child was untrue, that the couple were actually themselves 'party to keeping the child hidden as a tool of delaying deportation hearings'.

The second reason is five-and-a-half lines long, we cannot reveal what that reason is for even the released FBI document still has those five and a half lines blacked out (when a single line is blacked out that is only to be expected, the names and addresses of informants must, occasionally, be protected for 'national defence reasons' – when line after line goes missing it is much more sinister; even now, decades on, the truth is hidden from the public whose taxes paid for them).

The third reason stated is disturbing enough in itself, 'INS will request mental examinations of Lennons at later date...'.

Here was proof positive of the attitude behind the infamous John Dean memo of August 1971, wherein the President's counsel had gleefully stated that the machinery of government could be used 'to screw' political enemies. Here was the Nixon regime's hypocrisy laid bare. Having attacked the Soviets for using psychiatry to silence dissent, the US government was now suggesting 'mental examinations' could help deport a couple, a couple whose only real 'crime' had been criticising America's war in Vietnam.

There is something else interesting about this FBI wire, it, like many others later, specifically mentions that one of the FBI personnel to receive it is one ES Miller, head of the Domestic Intelligence Division and later to be one of the first two FBI agents convicted of crimes committed while on official FBI duty...

At the end of the hearings of 17 August Lennon said, 'I don't know if there's any mercy to plead for but, if so, I would like it for both us and our child.' A definite decision was again postponed but the Lennons were given leave to stay while this was happening.

On the following Saturday there was a 'Candlelight Vigil and Procession for Peace' in Duffy Square, New York ('Stop The Blockade Now! Stop The Bombing Now! US Out Of SE Asia Now!' read the flyers). Among those 'legally and peacefully' registering their opposition to 'Nixon's latest and most dangerous escalation' were satirist Jules Feiffer, actors Ben Gazzara, Viveca Lindfors, Eli Wallach, Lee Grant and Peter Boyle, writers Arthur Miller, Anaïs Nin and John Lahr...and, of course, John Lennon and Yoko Ono.

Sci-fi writer Kurt Vonnegut read out a statement, which concluded with the following thought: 'at this critical time, we believe it is important to share some time and peace and feeling for peace.' (In the small print of the previous day's newspaper stories – the actual headlines were reserved for news items on John and Yoko – lay the reason Nixon had resorted to ever more long-range bombing: both the troops in the field and at home were starting to rebel, even the US Servicemen's Fund was announcing a list of anti-war demonstrations at Fort Dix while New York's 23rd annual Armed Forces Parade had already been cancelled for fear of GI protests.)

Before the Lennons went back to their small Bank Street apartment that night they chatted to another celebrity who'd joined the protest – actor Robert Ryan. He was about to finish work on *Executive Action*, a new feature film he was appearing in alongside Burt Lancaster, Will Greer and John Anderson. It was being directed by David Miller and was based on Donald Freed and Mark Lane's best-selling book of the same name, a factional piece about the American intelligence services assassinating a popular liberal figure, namely President John F Kennedy...

The following week the FBI's Acting Director contacted his Houston office and boasted of the 'progress' being made in 'developing excellent coverage [of the] subject's activities, however, aspects investigation relating to subject's appearance at INS hearings and possible perjury involved in false statements made by subject strictly responsibility of INS...'.

When it came to proving that the Lennons had lied about Kyoko's whereabouts in Houston, 'in view of possible court proceedings active investigation by FBI in this area could result in FBI agents testifying which would not be in Bureau's best interest and could result in considerable adverse publicity...'.

The FBI didn't mind bugging and following the Lennons, going through their trash and trying to prove them liars...it just didn't want the public to know, in case of 'adverse publicity'. The Kyoko-in-Houston line of attack was all to be in vain anyway. The teletype of 25 May, despite having some 16 lines completely blanked out, ends mournfully, '...no further inquiry being made by Houston Division...'.

Meanwhile, a thousand miles away in the deep south of Atlanta, Georgia, a lonely 17-year-old-boy continued to nurse his biggest love – an ongoing obsession with the music and lyrics of one particular musician.

Mark David Chapman had not enjoyed his childhood. His father had been, in Chapman's opinion at least, cold and distant. His parents rowed, sometimes violently, while his mother would shelter in Mark's room as he got older. This undoubtedly helped to feed young Chapman's narcissistic tendencies – he was the equal, the helper of adults – as well as making him wary of male–female relationships (he was later to admit that he found the sexual act with women unappealing).

Chapman had taken strong LSD at 14 and been arrested the same year. He'd then run away to Miami for two weeks the next spring. After returning home, penniless, he'd enjoyed an intense but brief flirtation with religion. But even though he joined a Christian music group and organised special events for his local church, he continued to smoke dope and pop acid tabs.

By 1972 the teenager's main – some said his only – passions were drugs and the records of Todd Rundgren, the acerbic Philly-born singer/songwriter and producer. Rundgren, who'd had no success with his self-produced band Nazz, did clock up a Top 20 solo hit in 1970 with 'We've Gotta Get You A Woman', which appeared on Albert Grossman's Bearsville label.

Chapman had saved up and later bought that hit single, then the *Runt* album it came from and then the follow-up set (*The Ballad of Todd Rundgren*). Chapman was even said to have the *Straight Up* album Rundgren had produced for Badfinger, the Welsh band who'd been on The Beatles' Apple records. In 1972 Chapman's most treasured possession was Rundgren's double LP *Something/Anything?*, its smorgasbord of music styles – soul, semi-acoustic, heavy rock and pop – had a special appeal for a young man whose own life seemed to have been similarly scrambled...

13 Watching The Detectives

'An address book containing 395 entries was found...'
— FBI memo, May 1972

Although the now-ailing Hoover had told Nixon on 12 April 1972 that Lennon was only staying in the US in order to disrupt the forthcoming RNC, Lennon had actually abandoned such plans by then – he was too busy fighting deportation. Lennon's partial withdrawal from frontline politics was no doubt one intended side-effect of the CIA-FBI-INS crusade. It was an intense legal battle Lennon faced and even extreme radicals like Jerry Rubin understood Lennon's less involved position in the anti-war campaign, 'there was a child involved, after all'.

A coded FBI teletype was sent to the Director from the Bureau's New York field office on 3 May 1972. The teletype stated that the British government had 'advised' that Lennon's 1968 drugs conviction would not be 'overturned' no matter what – despite the subsequent prosecution of the arresting office Detective Sergeant Pilcher for 'perverting the course of justice'. Normally when a police officer is arrested, charged and convicted for breaking the law, all the previous cases he or she was in charge of are reviewed to see if any innocent person has been wrongly convicted in the past.

After being tipped off about Pilcher's interest Lennon had emptied the Montagu Square apartment of drugs, a clearout witnessed by Yoko Ono. Pilcher planted drugs there and was himself later jailed for dishonesty. So why wasn't Lennon's drugs case reviewed...?

On 12 May the INS had tried to divide the Lennons by granting Yoko, and Yoko alone, the right to stay longer (something she should have been given from the start – she hadn't been charged after Lennon's 1968

London bust, the official reason for keeping her husband out of the US).
To Lennon it must have seemed a provocation – whether he thought so
or not Lennon took to the streets the next day, supporting a New York
anti-war march and leading choruses of his 'Give Peace A Chance'.

It was 18 May that saw the sending of an FBI memo from SAC –
Special Agent in Charge of – Field Office San Diego to SAC NYC. It
speaks of the arrest of an unnamed – well, name deleted – anti-war activist
for 'Conspiracy to Injure Government Property and Trespassing for the
Purpose of Injuring Government Property during demonstrations against
the Vietnam War. An address book containing 395 entries was found in
his possession...'

Of the following three pages – which end with John and Yoko's
address – of these released Freedom of Information documents, virtually
three-quarters have been blanked out by the FBI on the grounds of
'national security'.

On 23 May an urgent teletype to the FBI's Acting Director still claimed
that Lennon intended 'to travel Republic and Democratic Convention
this year'.

Later, an unnamed officer of the 3rd Narcotics District, NYC 'advised
that his department had been unable to make a narcotics case on the
Lennons. NYPD continuing.'

In spite of all the lurid talk, and FBI memo references, the NYPD's
narcotics division had been unable to 'bust' Lennon for a single joint,
let alone with a stash of serious drugs. If the NYPD was serious about
catching law breakers, perhaps it should have been looking elsewhere.
Perhaps even in Washington DC...

A week later, press copies of Lennon's *Sometime In New York City*
album was issued, an abrasive collection of radical comments on current
causes – Lennon later admitted that 'the politics got in the way of the
poetry'. Although tracks like 'Woman Is The Nigger Of The World' do
break new ground – and rockers like 'New York City' still sound strong
– it is, in many ways, just like the newspaper the album cover parodies,
artistically a snapshot of a man on the run...

Astonishingly, just weeks later Nixon's Attorney General Mitchell
did agree to the illegal E Howard Hunt and Gordon Liddy scheme – to

break in and bug the Democrat HQ within Washington DC's Watergate complex. It was to be charged to CREEP – the Committee to Re-Elect the President. Barker was put in charge of the burglary and took along Hunt, Sturgis and two others on the evening of 16 June 1972...

Some two weeks later – with talk of the Watergate burglary raising awkward questions – John Lennon met several 'radical journalists'. He is said to have offered both encouragement and money to aid their attempt to expose the Nixon links with the burglars (the details of exactly when and where the meeting took place now seem to be lost but it is a known fact that Lennon was intensely interested in the Watergate case and he did actually attend at least one of the Washington DC Watergate hearings – on 29 June 1973).

Several months later, as *Washington Post* reporters Woodward and Bernstein fought editorial indifference and neared the heart of the Watergate story, their inside source, 'Deep Throat', told them that their lives were in danger – on 8 December 1972, E Howard Hunt's wife, another woman linked to US intelligence, died after the plane she was on blew up when it was several miles high over Chicago airport; earlier in the year Hunt had refused a request, from Nixon aide Charles Colson, to break into Arthur Bremer's house after Bremer had attempted to assassinate rightist presidential candidate George Wallace of Alabama.

The 21-year-old Bremer had fired five shots from a .38 at Wallace at close range. Within seconds he was overcome and arrested; the subsequent wounding of Wallace prevented him running for the 1972 presidency, thus giving Nixon the entire right and far right vote – and victory. (In May 1972, at Nixon's request, the FBI had sealed Bremer's residence, preventing local police from investigating further...)

On 8 December 1972 the New York SAC sent an Airtel, SUBJECT: JOHN LENNON, to the Acting Director, copies of which were to go on to the US Legat in London. It stated that 'in view of subject's inactivity in Revolutionary Activities and his seeming rejection by NY Radicals, captioned case is being closed in the NY Division.

'In the event other information comes to New York's attention indicating subject is active with Revolutionary groups, the case will be re-opened at that time and the Bureau advised accordingly.'

With Nixon successfully re-elected, the Vietnam War still on and Lennon still busy struggling against deportation, the FBI decided – officially at least – to close the John Lennon file.

The fact that only four CIA John Lennon documents have ever been seen publicly – when it's known there are dozens, perhaps hundreds, more – is not exactly reassuring. Nor is the fact that over a dozen of the available FBI pages are mostly or completely blacked out – others have two- or three-line deletions and others still have sneaky 'white-outs' that are even harder to see or track down. At least one other even has its date censored and could have been sent at any point between 1968 and 1981 (it is a 'Foreign Government Information' document, one that relates to the country of the former Beatles' birth – Great Britain).

And yet, all in all, it is likely that the FBI *did* relax its surveillance of Lennon a little after Nixon's November 1972 victory, as the December Airtel outlines. Exactly how long that stand-down actually lasted no outsider really knows…

14 The Lost Weekend

'I'm all in favour of it, either booze or religion, whatever gets you
through the damn night'

– Frank Sinatra

On US election night 1972, as state after state voted for Nixon, an
increasingly depressed Lennon began to hit the bottle like a man on a
mission. By 9:30pm he was openly flirting with other women in front
of Yoko, by midnight he was groping them. A bad year was coming to
a bad end. The Lennons still hadn't got John's green card, nor had they
got a hit album – *Sometime In New York City* had failed to reach the
US Top 40 – and nor, more importantly, did they have the full-term
pregnancy Yoko had been seeking for over three years.

New Year 1973 seemed to continue the trend, the couple quarrelling
while Yoko's ground breaking *Approximately Infinite Universe* album
failed to reach the Top 100. The pressure of fighting eviction from the
US, a battle now well over a year old, was starting to tell.

Early March, however, saw Lennon having a little fun unofficially
producing Ringo's new album in LA. George Harrison dropped down
later, at Lennon's invitation, and for a few carefree hours there was almost
a Beatles reunion happening.

The party mood ended abruptly on 23 March when Lennon was
given a 'full and final' order to leave the United States of America within
60 days or face arrest and deportation. Lennon's wife was given permission
to stay indefinitely. In April, after hiring ABKCO beauty May Pang as
an in-house assistant, the Lennons moved into the Upper West Side
Manhattan building that actor Robert Ryan, now dying of cancer, had
first introduced them to – the exclusive Dakota on 72nd Street.

With the 'final' deportation just weeks away, John Lennon's attorney Leon Wildes managed to win yet another postponement.

At the end of June, John and Yoko made one of their last public political gestures – joining a demonstration at the South Vietnamese Embassy in Washington DC to protest about the Saigon regime's imprisonment of a female Buddhist peace activist. A photo of the Lennons at the South Vietnamese Embassy was copied to the FBI Washington Field Office file on Lennon that summer (if the FBI had definitely closed Lennon's file it had a funny way of showing it).

The next day, whilst still in DC, the Lennons attended the Watergate Hearings, now in full flow as Nixon and his cronies fought to keep the power they had so blatantly abused.

A 25 September 1973 FBI missive headed 'ELECTRONIC SURVEILLANCE' claims that, after studying records concerning captioned individual Lennon, it had been discovered that he was 'not the subject of a direct electronic surveillance nor were any of [his] conversations monitored by an electronic device of the FBI'.

Which isn't to say that, even if this were true, local police intelligence units couldn't have carried out similar wire-taps. So could the CIA and so could other pan-state agencies. The letter half acknowledges this by blandly ending, 'it is suggested that other Federal investigative agencies be contacted to determine if they had coverage of the subject(s)'.

There is no evidence that the suggestion was acted on or that any such checks took place. Federal bugging of the Lennons *had* happened – far too many callers had heard the clicks and conversation replays that were then the hallmarks of phone bugging – but now it was being discussed in public, no one in authority was anxious to find a smoking gun – especially if it might turn out to be in their own pocket. Such a result would be bad, to say the least, for US intelligence 'unity'.

John and Yoko's own united public front couldn't last, however, and with Yoko said to be dating David Spinozza, Lennon recorded the *Mind Games* album at New York's Record Plant before taking off with May Pang the same month as the FBI's mealy-mouthed electronic surveillance letter. According to May, during Lennon's time with her – the 15 months up to February 1975 – he didn't worry about the FBI at all.

'He was well aware of his immigration status, but he didn't think he was being followed [then]…John loved being in the studio, but he felt safe virtually everywhere,' she insists. 'He was very down to earth and didn't project any energy that might be negative. At most, he'd have to sign an autograph, shake a hand or pose for a picture, which he gladly did when he either arrived or left the studio…prior to December 1980, I don't believe any rock star felt really "at-risk". People were very cool, very friendly to both of us and gave us our space. Nor did I ever feel I was in danger…He took the immigration battle seriously, he just didn't understand why the United States government thought he was so important… During our time together, he was enjoying life and making music…he was very proud of his [solo] success; he was a humble man and it actually surprised him, having his first Number One single and album. He was also very happy re-establishing ties with Julian.'

Lennon's time with Pang, while no doubt enjoyable in the main, was not all sweetness and light however. Drink was flowing at too fast a rate and Lennon, with boozer Harry Nilsson in attendance, even managed to get thrown out of a few clubs and bars.

Recording the *Rock 'n' Roll* album with Phil Spector was similarly wild, with Lennon drunkenly trashing Lou Adler's memorabilia collection. The recording sessions themselves quickly ground to a complete halt after wall-of-sound man Phil let off guns in the live room before, reportedly, taking a dump in one of the elevators.

On 1 March Lennon appeared before the INS again to appeal against the latest US government deportation order, then flew back to May Pang in Hollywood – there Elizabeth Taylor introduced him to David Bowie. Despite the worst fears of both, the Man Who Fell to Earth and the former Beatle actually got on.

After more drunken high jinks with Nilsson – and Ringo and Keith Moon – Lennon returned to New York on 18 July in time for the INS to slap another 'final 60 day' quit order on him. He returned to court on 31 August to claim that he'd been denied the right to stay in the United States purely on political grounds, because Nixon feared that he would campaign heavily against the president in the run-up to the 1972 election.

With Nixon having been forced to resign over Watergate just three weeks before there finally seemed to be a slight chance that Lennon's 'green card quest' might yet succeed.

Amid the 1974 mayhem Lennon clocked his first solo US Number One hit – 'Whatever Gets You Through The Night' (the title was taken from one of Sinatra's oft-repeated throwaway lines when he was with Mia Farrow, 'I'm all in favour of it, either booze or religion, whatever gets you through the damn night', which came complete with choruses backed by Elton John and reached the top in November just as his new *Walls And Bridges* album managed the same feat.

Fulfilling an old promise, Lennon appeared onstage at an Elton John gig before 20,000 people at Madison Square Gardens – he and Elton performed Lennon's current Number One plus 'Lucy In The Sky With Diamonds' and 'I Saw Her Standing There'. Lennon and Yoko chatted backstage afterwards – their first face-to-face for many months.

With the New Year's Day hangover still ringing in his head, Lennon went to court yet again – but this time to be told by Judge Richard Owen that he should be allowed to interview INS officials and even to inspect their files on him in order to see whether political considerations had played any part in their persecution of him.

A fortnight later Lennon accepted Bowie's invitation to join the *Young Americans* album sessions. Lennon was mainly there as an observer but he contributed to a interesting cover of The Beatles' 'Across The Universe' before, with Bowie and guitarist Carlos Alomar, cooking up a 'clunky yet funky' guitar riff. 'Worra great riff, wow, worra great riff that is,' Lennon eulogised before suggesting the title 'Fame' – it became one of Bowie's finest tracks, with the Thin White Duke's lyrics dissecting a subject Lennon knew all too well: the problems and pressures of fame.

In mid February Yoko contacted him about a new anti-smoking cure she felt he should try. Within weeks the Lennons were reunited and soon, after using a diet suggested by a Chinese acupuncturist, Yoko shocked everyone by becoming pregnant.

The Lennons' TV friend Geraldo Rivera later shocked America, on 6 March 1975, with 26 seconds of eight-millimetre film screened on his NBC *Good Night America* show.

The Zapruder home-movie footage was of the JFK assassination, the only clear film that the FBI or Warren Commission would admit existed of the killing. Outside of the FBI and Warren Commissioners, only amateur cameraman Abe Zapruder and CBS TV reporter Dan Rather had seen the footage. Rather had described it as showing JFK being knocked *forwards* as he is killed. Selected frames printed in *Life* magazine supported this – *Life* had bought the rights from Zapruder – which seemed to confirm the 'lone-nut theory', that Lee Harvey Oswald had killed JFK alone, firing three shots from behind the president.

But *Life* was published by Henry Luce whose wife Clare Booth Luce was an anti-Castro fanatic who had little time for Kennedy. And both *Life* and Rather had *not* told the truth. After photo-analyst Bob Groden had given a Zapruder film copy to Dick Gregory – the entertainer and civil rights activist who was another Lennon friend – the latter had persuaded Rivera to screen it live on network TV.

Here for the first time the America public got to see the footage that the federal authorities had been hiding for over a decade – colour film that clearly showed JFK's fatal wound coming from the *front*. *Life* had cheated the film-frame sequence and Oswald had obviously not acted alone. America's intelligence services had lied all along – there *had* been a conspiracy, after all.

In March 1975 one committed, right-wing Christian, the 20-year-old Mark David Chapman, used a YMCA international scheme to apply to visit the Sovet Union. It seemed a strange choice – why go somewhere that you do not like or approve of?

When this Russian visit fell through – through Chapman's lack of Russian language skills – he had then picked the potential troublespot known as Beirut (which had seen shootings and massacres for months).

Chapman *could* have chosen to go Jerusalem, Bethlehem or Nazareth – these were ancient Holy Land places of interest to anyone with a spiritual bent, let alone a Christian.

Yet Chapman chose Beirut and was at that city's YMCA in June 1975 during the first few bloody weeks of the Lebanese civil war – later, after he and the other YMCA visitors were pulled out, Chapman played his friends tapes of the gunfire. He also wrote a letter to the YMCA's South

De Kalb Board of Management. In the letter he admitted to being thrilled by his little excursion.

None of this is logical if Chapman is merely an innocent traveller – a Christian tries to visit the Soviet Union? Then goes to the Middle East but avoids the holy places? And all in preference for a troublespot that had became a war zone? He wasn't doing charity or medical work there. So why?

There is one other point that should be mentioned about Beirut: it was a major base for CIA and US Naval Intelligence right up until the '80s. Beirut was also for years said to have been the home of a top-secret assassination training camp...

On 23 April 1975 the South Vietnamese regime finally crumbled as desperate southern officials tried to hold on to the US helicopters taking off from Saigon's US Embassy. Within hours the Americans were gone and the Vietnam War was finally over – most western reporters fled as well, fearing that the North Vietnamese, and the few surviving VC, would instigate a massacre. Their fears turned out to be groundless, despite some harassment of 'collaborators' there was no bloodbath as the two Vietnams finally became one.

Five days later Lennon gave his last major TV interview, with lawyer Leon Wildes and host Tom Snyder on NBC. On 19 June Lennon filed suits against both Richard Kleindienst and Nixon's former Attorney General John Mitchell – his suits claiming that both men deliberately blocked Lennon's US visa application for purely political reasons.

With the Zapruder assassination film out in the open – and following the Watergate and Vietnamese 'defeats' – pressure grew for an inquiry into America's intelligence services. The Frank Church Committee and House Select Committee on Assassinations (HSCA) freed thousands of documents revealing numerous FBI and CIA crimes, lies and distortions. Acoustic experts conducting tests on Dallas sound tapes of 22 November 1963 concluded on behalf of the HSCA that at least four shots were fired. Even when the HSCA was 'neutered' by new chairman Robert Blakey its official conclusion was still front-page news – there *was* a conspiracy to kill John F Kennedy. But Blakey's committee refused to point a definite finger of blame beyond murmurings about the Mafia.

After Oliver Stone's 1992 movie *JFK* showed the Zapruder film again, amid much new factional detail, there was a further demand for information – the government's subsequent JFK Act allowed thousands more pages to become public, including some that showed that the '50s and early '60s income-tax records of Lee Harvey Oswald and one of his relatives were classified as 'state secrets' of the highest order.

There were also two other individuals whose '50s and early '60s income tax records were considered so important that they too were now 'state secrets' of the highest order. In fact, these individuals were – are – so important to some arm of the US state that, over 30 years later, the public are not even allowed to know their initials, let alone their full names. Researchers who had previously been sceptical about the Oswald lookalike theory were forced to think again. Who were these unnamed two? And why did their secret tax records shadow those of the Oswalds?

The year 1975 ended on a high for the Lennons – as Bowie got his first US Number One, with the Lennon co-composition 'Fame', the INS was finally forced to give some ground as a federal court, on behalf of the New York State Senate, cancelled the original John Lennon deportation order and insisted that the INS reconsider Lennon's request for full resident status. The elusive green card had moved a few inches closer.

Lennon was still smiling two days later when, on his own birthday, 9 October, Yoko gave birth to Sean Taro Ono Lennon. The couple's joy was mingled with fear over Yoko's health following the traumatic Caesarian birth but, after two weeks, she and the child were thought well enough to be allowed home to the Dakota Building.

At the same time, Mark David Chapman finished several months of working with Vietnamese refugees at the camp in Fort Chaffee, Arkansas. He had been flown there a few weeks after returning from his three-week trip to Beirut…

For John Lennon, New Year 1976 started bleakly – his old friend, and much-loved Beatles aide, Mal Evans was shot and killed by LA police officers after allegedly threatening his girlfriend with a gun. On hearing the news Lennon wept.

Three months later another Lennon friend was the target as fellow rock star David Bowie was involved in a major police drugs bust in

New York State – unfortunately for the Westchester police all they could find amongst the possessions of Bowie and his entourage was a small amount of marijuana.

But Bowie and two of his friends were still arrested and charged. He was then bailed for thousands of dollars and had to appear before the same court in March 1977 (but by then the Nixon-Ford years were finally over and Democrat Jimmy Carter was in the White House – the Bowie prosecution was quietly dropped…).

On 27 July 1976, as *Melody Maker* hailed the new English punk bands who would apparently 'inspire' a third generation of rockers, Lennon's five-year legal battle reached its conclusion.

The hearing was at New York's Immigration Bureau. After opening statements, Lennon – supported by the likes of writer Norman Mailer, actress Gloria Swanson and TV personality Geraldo Rivera – took the stand and was asked a series of questions by Leon Wildes.

> LW: Have you ever been convicted of any crime, anywhere in the USA?
> JL: No.
> LW: Have you ever been a member of the Communist Party or any other organization that may seek to overthrow the US government by force?
> JL: No.
> LW: Do you intend to make the US your home?
> JL: I do.

Minutes later Norman Mailer took the oath. 'I think John Lennon is a great artist who has made an enormous contribution to popular culture,' said America's finest living novelist before adding, 'he is one of the great artists of the western world. We lost TS Eliot to England and only got Auden back…'.

After the Bishop of New York called Lennon 'a gentleman of integrity', Gloria Swanson spoke up as well, praising the ex-Beatle for his 'anti-junk food' attitude – she'd met him in a health food store chasing after macrobiotic fare – a positive notion, which she thought he could spread to a wider public.

After 90 minutes Lennon was at last told he'd be given his own green card (except that, like most 'green' cards then, this one was actually blue). Judge Ira Fieldsteel announced the verdict and the Lennons smiled as the rest of the court-room spontaneously burst into applause. Now the Dakota's most famous resident could come and go – and remain – within the US indefinitely.

'It's great to be legal again!' a smiling Lennon told TV reporters afterwards, 'the Immigration Service have finally seen the light of day. Its been a long and slow road but I'm not bitter. On the contrary, now I can go and visit my relatives in Japan and elsewhere…'.

Will you now go on and become a full US citizen, one journalist asked?

'I wanna enjoy the advantages of holding a green card before I make up my mind on that point. The main thing is I can travel now. Until today my attorney wouldn't even let me go to Hawaii for a vacation in case I couldn't get back in. Whenever I flew to Los Angeles I was paranoid in case the plane was diverted to Toronto on the way.'

When asked why he'd chosen to live in New York anyway, Lennon replied: 'If I had lived two thousand years ago I would have wanted to live in Rome. New York is the Rome of today…now I'm going home to crack open a tea-bag and start looking at some travelogues!'

He could also have said, as he did both before and after, that he loved the exhilarating buzz of New York – Greenwich Village and SoHo and the sites that Yoko had first discovered as a teenager – a city where the people in the streets didn't ever 'hassle you' (although it was in New York that Lennon first started to dream about a stranger who asked for an album autograph then returned later, angry and with a loaded gun…).

The very last question Wildes had asked Lennon that day was to the point: do you wish to continue your work here? To which Lennon had replied, 'Yes, I wish to continue to live here with my family and to continue making music.' But this wasn't quite the case – for the next three and a half years there would be precious little music made by either Lennon or Yoko and none for scheduled release. Nor would his relatives 'elsewhere' – Aunt Mimi and the others back in Britain – ever receive another visit. Lennon would not live to see England again.

In January 1977 Chapman arrived in Hawaii. Some later claimed he'd gone there to committ suicide, others that he just wanted to get away from his family and friends, and still others said he was feeling just fine at that point.

The Hawaiian islands were then – and to an extent still are now – a tropical paradise, with extinct volcanoes providing the perfect backdrop to endless sun-kissed beaches fringed with palms. The islands bristle with golf courses, exclusive clubs and five-star hotels.

They are also home to a US Naval Intelligence complex and at least seven US Naval and Army bases. And Hawaii, like Chapman's other old stamping ground Beirut, is also – according to Daniel Sheehan of the Christic Institute – the site of a top-secret assassination training camp, owned and used by US intelligence.

After arriving at Honolulu airport Chapman checked in to the expensive Moana Hotel, money again seemingly no object. After a few weeks he returned to Georgia, then flew back and stayed in the local Honolulu YMCA.

A year of dead-end jobs led to Chapman's alleged suicide attempt. Whether it was a genuine effort or not, Chapman had soon checked in to the psychiatric wing of Castle Memorial Hospial. Within weeks Chapman – his suicide 'attempt' all but forgotten – was observing mentally ill patients as he started work for the Castle Doctors (one of the fastest turnarounds in psychiatric history).

In July 1978, after arranging a complex itinerary with his travel agent, a pretty Japanese-American girl called Gloria, Chapman took off on a world tour. It is an amazing trip for a college dropout without independent wealth, encompassing as it does the most expensive cities on Earth: Tokyo in Japan, London in England and Geneva in Switzerland.

Then there are the weeks he spent in India and Nepal, where he caused a riot with his useless gesture of giving box after box of chewing gum to hungry street kids. There was also Bangkok in Thailand – even then a favourite holiday destination for sex tourists of all appetites – plus Hong Kong, Korea and two communist destinations.

Vietnam and China had just started to allow a few western tourists in at that point, so Chapman became one of the very first to see Red

China and unified Vietnam (perhaps it made up for his failed attempt to get into Soviet Russia in 1975). He then flew on to Iran.

These were just some of the countries Chapman visited while he snapped away with his camera – taking over 1,200 Kodachrome colour slides. On the way back to Hawaii, Chapman changed planes and flew to Atlanta so he could call in on his police friend Dana Reeves.

When Chapman finally got back to Honolulu on 20 August, travel agent Gloria Abe was waiting for him at the airport. They would be wed within the year.

15 Watching The Wheels (1979)

'When I did 'Woman Is The Nigger Of The World' I was a feminist
in theory, only later did I really become one.'

– *John Lennon*

A Love Letter From John And Yoko To People Who Ask Us What, When, Why:
'The past ten years we noticed everything we wished came true
in its own time, good or bad, one way or the other. We kept
telling each other that one of these days we would have to get
organized and wish for only good things. Then our baby
arrived! We were overjoyed and at the same time felt very
responsible. Now our wishes would also affect him. We felt it
was time for us to stop discussing and do something about our
wishing process: The Spring Cleaning of our minds! It was a
lot of work. We kept finding things in those old closets that,
in our minds, we hadn't realised were still there, things we
wished we hadn't found.

As we did our cleaning we also started to notice many
wrong things in our house: there was a shelf which should never
have been there in the first place, a painting we grew to dislike,
and there were the dingy rooms, which became light and breezy
when we broke the walls between them. We started to love the
plants, which one of us originally thought were robbing the air
from us! We began to enjoy the drum beat of the city which
used to annoy us. We made a lot of mistakes and still do. In the
past we spent a lot of energy trying to get something we thought
we wanted, we wondered why we didn't get it, only to find out
that one or both of us didn't really want it.

One day we received a sudden rain of chocolates from people round the world. "Hey, what's this! We're not eating sugar stuff, are we?"

"Who's wishing it?" We both laughed.

We discovered that when two of us wished in unison, it happened faster. As the Good Book says – Where two are gathered together: It's true. Two is plenty. A Newclear Seed.

More and more we are starting to wish and pray. The things we have tried to achieve in the past by flashing a V sign, we try now through wishing. We are not doing this because it's simpler. Wishing is more effective than waving flags. It works. It's like magic. Magic is simple. Magic is real. The secret of it is to know that it is simple, and not kill it with an elaborate ritual which is a sign of insecurity. When somebody is angry with us, we draw a halo around his or her head in our minds. Does this person stop being angry then? Well, we don't know! We know, though, that when we draw a halo around a person, suddenly the person starts to look like an angel to us. This helps us to feel warm towards the person, reminds us that everyone has goodness inside, and that all people who come to us are angels in disguise, carrying messages and gifts to us from the Universe. Magic is logical. Try it sometime.

We still have a long way to go. It seems the more we get into cleaning, the faster the wishing and receiving process gets. The house is getting very comfortable now. Sean is beautiful. The plants are growing. The cats are purring. The town is shining, sun, rain or snow. We live in a beautiful universe. We are thankful everyday for the plentifulness of our life. This is not a euphemism. We understand that, we, the city, the country, the earth are facing very hard times and there is a panic in the air. Still the sun is shining and we are here together, and there is love between us, our city, the country, the earth. If two people like us can do what we are doing with our lives, any miracle is possible! It's true we can do with a few big miracles right now. The thing is to recognise them when they come to you and be thankful. First they come in a small way, in everyday life, then they come in rivers, and in oceans. It's goin' to be alright! The future of the earth is up to all of us.

Many people are sending us vibes everyday in letters, telegrams, taps on the gate, or just flowers and nice thoughts. We thank them all and appreciate them for respecting our quiet space, which we need. Thank you for all the love you send us. We feel it every day. We love you too. We know you are concerned about us. That is nice. That's why you want to know what we are doing. That's why everybody is asking us What, When and Why. We understand. Well, this is what we're doing. We hope that you have the same quiet space in your mind to make your own wishes come true.

If you think of us next time, remember, our silence is a silence of love and not of indifference. Remember, we are writing in the sky instead of on paper – that's our song. Lift your eyes and look up in the sky. There's our message. Lift your eyes again and look around you, and you will see that you are walking in the sky, which extends to the ground. We are all part of the sky, more so than of the ground. Remember, we love you.'

John Lennon and Yoko Ono
27 May 1979
New York City

Although at times banal to the critical eye, the Lennons' May 1979 advert-stroke-letter to *The New York Times* does have a certain spaced-out charm all its own – a missive that's a blend of prototype New Age mysticism and rock rebel royalty tips, affectionately passed on in maturity to those who might not know.

Superficially at least, on first reading, it comes across as a gentle letter of resignation both from music and any kind of political involvement. The line 'when you think of us' almost begs to be followed by the words, 'please remember the good times...'.

But there's happiness there too – a genuine celebration of little Sean.

In terms of perfect domestic bliss he may have arrived six or seven years behind schedule yet it's always better late than never with a child – and there seems a real joy about the couple's words after he's mentioned.

The talk of magic and prayer was also appropriate. The man who'd sang about there being 'no heaven' was now a firm believer in an after-life. 'You *do* go on,' he'd said to several friends and acquaintances, 'it's just like changing your suit or your car, it's a change but you do go on.' He seemed quite certain about it.

For the three years following the 1976 court victory Lennon had stayed in. He wasn't quite the hermit of legend – he still sometimes strolled to the coffee shop round the corner and there were also visits to Japan, Spain and – some claimed – South Africa. But though he doodled with songs, there were no serious, full-on recording sessions. Lennon even let his recording contracts lapse. For the first time in 18 years he had no record label.

'I think he'd genuinely got to a point in his life when he was happy,' says Roy Carr, an occasional New York visitor in the days before 1980. 'He wasn't out partying. You used to have to phone there and leave a message for "Johnny Rhythm". And then an hour or two later he'd usually call you back at your hotel and say "c'mon on over". And he'd be sitting there, asking if you'd seen any good Beatles gear, watching the news or The Beatles cartoons – he loved those cartoons. Having got out and survived it, I think he'd got it all in perspective by then. He could look back and see that there had been plenty of good times.'

A serious Beatles reunion still seemed to be a no-no though. 'What would we do? Play "Twist And Shout"? The Beatles were only really The Beatles in Liverpool and Hamburg anyway. After that it was just showbiz.'

To all intents and purposes Lennon had retired, happy to play the househusband while Yoko did deals on real estate and re-releases...

On 4 November 1979 the post-Shah Iran finally erupted against the symbol of the country that had most blatantly supported him and his hated secret police. The US Embassy was stormed by militant students and dozens of US officials were taken hostage. The officials' last few hours' work – shredding thousands of State Department and CIA documents – was undone as the young Tehran radicals swiftly set up special 'de-shredding' centres where, on the floors of gyms and basketball pitches, most of the papers were painstakingly re-assembled by carpet-weavers, pieced together over a period of weeks.

The exiled Shah had flown to New York for medical treatment just ten days before – the loss of 'his' country no doubt aggravating his cancer condition.

But 1979 was a bad year all round for dictators. The genocidal Stalinist regime of Pol Pot, although still discreetly backed by the US and recognised by the UN, collapsed after Hanoi – angered by years of border incidents – ordered a full-scale Vietnamese invasion of Cambodia (the successful invasion revealed the full horror of Pot's Khmer Rouge 'killing fields' for the first time – over a million civilians had been murdered there, their skulls heaped up into two-storey pyramids...).

Nicaragua's hated 'el hefe' Somoza killed thousands of opposition activists but he and his National Guard thugs were eventually forced from power that year by the leftist Sandinistas; the latter started a new government that contained businessmen, poets and priests (elements within the US media and Congress immediately condemned the new regime as 'communistic').

In central Africa, Islamic dictator Jean-Bedel Bokassa – infamous for the armed 'woman hunts' he took French officials on – and Uganda's cannibal president Idi Amin were both ejected from power in popular revolutions.

In post-Franco Spain, Adolfo Suarez became the nation's first elected prime minister for 43 years, and civilian rule was restored to Nigeria.

Before the year was out, though, the colonels in El Salvador had killed 60 civilian demonstrators and launched another coup. Meanwhile, thousands of miles away, the Russians responded to the growing, CIA-sponsored chaos in neighbouring Afghanistan by sending in an invasion force – a leading member of President Carter's cabinet, Zbigniew Brzezinski, is said to have cheered at the news, glad that the Soviets had taken the bait: 'Now we can give 'em [the Russians] their own Vietnam!'

16 Walking On Thin Ice

'It's up to all of us to make what we can of the '80s.'
– John Lennon

On 29 September 1980, *Newsweek* broke the story that had been an open secret in the US music industry for much of the preceding week – John Lennon's comeback was official. A new album, *Double Fantasy*, was mentioned as was the forthcoming single, '(Just Like) Starting Over'. These recordings, credited to both John and Yoko, were mostly started in Bermuda in June 1980. Others were based on sketches begun years before, though this doesn't necessarily mean, however, that the Lennons' talk of a totally fresh album was hyperbole: the completion of the songs, the end production, the ultimate arrangements and the final flourishes were all new, as were, of course, the mixes (and mixing and production are, since *Sergeant Pepper*, a key part of every audio release).

Sneak previews of the recordings were – like the finished reviews later – mixed. But the album did contain work as good as anything Lennon had ever recorded. Apart from the jaunty '50s parody 'Starting Over' and funky 'Clean-Up Time' other highlights included the moody 'I'm Losing You', the touching 'Woman' and the superb, uncluttered 'Watching The Wheels' – the latter perhaps being the perfect pop single even though it broke some of the rules that Lennon himself had helped to write (the first chorus doesn't come in until the song's halfway through...).

Ono's contribution is more problematic for most critics, though 'Beautiful Boys', her ode to her son and husband, shows her ability – rarely used it must be said – to marry both western and Japanese musical traditions to great effect. It is a true family album, an authentic marriage of different genres, cultures, styles, poems, egos...

Lennon's own song dedicated to four-year-old Sean, the similarly titled 'Beautiful Boy' is superbly produced, with its discreet 'vocoded' backing vocals on the chorus and Lennon's paternal whispers. It is intensely poignant – within a month of its release it is to become unbearably so...

According to his post-9 December recollections, Mark David Chapman decided that Barbara Graustark's *Newsweek* story of 29 September revealed Lennon as 'phoney'. The disillusioned 'life-long fan' then, he later said, played all his old Beatles and Lennon records. To Chapman, they showed Lennon's 'hypocrisy' at its most obvious. The fanatically 'devout' fan suddenly became Lennon's enemy – though murder had not yet entered his mind, he says.

All of which would be fine except for several points – Graustark's story was *not* remotely hostile to the Lennons. And besides all that, Chapman had never, ever been a real Beatles or Lennon fan.

To the Reverend Newton Hendrix, who'd been in the high school choir with him, Chapman 'never' expressed any comment at all about the band or Lennon. Nor did Hendrix ever hear Chapman sing 'Imagine if John Lennon was dead!', the perverted rewrite of 'Imagine' that Chapman was alleged to have sung over and over again at Hendrix's prayer group meetings.

Nor were any of Chapman's few original songs done in a style that even vaguely resembled anything done by The Beatles or Lennon.

Captain Louis Souza of the Honolulu police spent the period between mid December 1980 and mid January 1981 thoroughly investigating Chapman and his background. He was later to tell barrister and journalist Fenton Bresler that Chapman was not a Lennon fan. As far as Souza and his officers could discover, Chapman hadn't put forward 'any' opinions whatsoever about Lennon.

In fact, as discussed earlier, the only musician that Chapman had ever really expressed any admiration for, from way back in 1972, was Todd Rundgren, whose work had sometimes moved him to tears.

Chapman's Beatles and Lennon 'collection' was never photographed or catalogued and the 14 hours of cassette tapes that some reports claim he later had with him were never produced.

When, between 20 and 22 October 1980, Chapman wanted to listen to Lennon records he had, by his own admission, to go to the Honolulu Public Library to hear them *as he had none of his own.*

When, within 24 hours of this, he wanted to hear some Beatles' tracks he had to dig out some of his wife's Beatles albums *since, again, he had none of his own.* Admittedly, Chapman and his siblings had once owned a copy of *Meet The Beatles* – but so had over 3 million other American families. And, besides, that was over 15 years before, back in the autumn of 1964 when Chapman was barely nine. And it was the only feeble connection with what was supposed to be the biggest thing in his life.

This point just cannot be stressed too much; despite all the subsequent press hype, the plain fact is that Mark David Chapman, the supposed 'John Lennon obsessive', the 'fan of fans', owned not a single one of Lennon's records until he bought a copy of *Double Fantasy* during the last weekend of Lennon's life. Not one. Some 'fan', some 'obsession'...

On 2 October 1980, at Washington DC's L'Enfant Plaza Hotel, an Iranian said to be an intermediary for the new Tehran regime met three officials from presidential candidate Ronald Reagan's campaign team. There was no press conference – the meeting was top secret. Two weeks later Reagan's men met more Iranians, this time in Paris. Although candidate Reagan was leading Democrat President Carter in virtually all the polls, the men behind the right-wing Republican Reagan were taking no chances – they knew the main reason for Carter's unpopularity was his inability to get the American hostages in Iran home.

The Reagan men needed this 'hostage crisis' situation to continue until the day after the election and preferably until Reagan's presidential inauguration. So they, it is alleged, offered the Iranians a deal – over $3 million cash and the promise of resumed US arms sales to Iran after Reagan's electoral victory. But if, and only if, Tehran delayed the release of the American hostages until January. The Iranians allegedly said the offer was acceptable.

There appear to be no surviving records of either of these meetings, but both Carter's CIA Director Admiral Stansfield Turner – and his White House press secretary, Jody Powell – are just two of many who are absolutely convinced that they took place.

On 29 October Chapman flew from Honolulu to New York, carrying with him a .38 handgun. He stood outside the Dakota for much of the next day and for the following five, but the staff continued to tell him Lennon was away.

The day after Reagan's electoral victory Chapman flew off to Georgia where his longtime associate Dana Reeves, an Atlanta police officer, had no qualms about supplying him with five deadly hollow-point bullets (mutual acquaintances have since described Reeves as being a 'bad influence' on Chapman and the latter seems to have been intimidated by him, a single glance from Reeves apparently being enough to make Mark freeze in his tracks).

On 9 November Chapman took yet another plane – money seemingly no object for the unemployed former security guard – and arrived back in New York. He returned to his Dakota vigil for three days then – after allegedly wrestling with his mysterious 'kill Lennon compulsion' – he phoned his wife before flying back to Hawaii on 12 November...

On 28 November John Lennon, as part of the legal effort to stop the stage show *Beatlemania*, signed an affidavit stating that the four former Beatles had agreed to reunite for a concert during the next five years.

December 1980 started with a pleasant surprise for some Japanese-American workers involved in a strike against their food-importing employers on the West Coast (the bosses were insisting on paying them less than their white American co-workers) – a supportive telegram arrived from New York.

'We are with you in spirit. Both of us are subjected to prejudice and abuse as an Oriental family in the Western world. Boycott it must be, if it is the only way to bring justice and restore the dignity of the constitution for the sake of all citizens of the US and their children. Peace and love.'

John Lennon and Yoko Ono,
New York City, December 1980'

But, to the workers' astonishment, they discover that the Lennons weren't just going to support their boycott of the companies in question, they were coming over – John, Yoko and little Sean – in mid-December to San Francisco. The Lennons were actually going to march alongside the strikers and their families.

There were now even rumours that the former Beatle would attend an anti-nukes demo in the New Year. John Lennon wasn't just back on the music scene, he was starting to re-enter politics again – and damn the fact that Reagan was now president-elect.

Reagan's electoral victory had been a major slap in the face to most American liberals – and to the vast majority of Europeans. Reagan's main political mentor had been his father-in-law, who'd constantly raged about the pernicious influence of 'niggers' and 'kikes', and similar attitudes lurked amongst some of his kitchen cabinet. Reasonable people asked how could the man who'd supported McCarthy over the Red witchhunts in the '50s, Goldwater over the Vietnam War in the '60s and Nixon over Watergate in the '70s now be president-elect of the United States of America?

Reagan's victory was mainly, of course, down to Carter's failure to get the US hostages out of Iran. Although Carter, to be fair, had tried almost everything, including a military helicopter getaway that had gone wrong in very bizarre circumstances – chopper after chopper crashing into each other as if sabotaged, leaving over a dozen US personnel dead...

Whoever was to blame it still left Reagan – the man who'd once compared JFK with Hitler, the man who'd held a cocktail party the weekend of Kennedy's funeral – as leader of the free world. A man in his 70s, many of whose supporters believed in 'the rapture' – wherein born-again Christians would suddenly be 'raptured', taken out of this sinful 'half-communistic' world and placed in the next. Others, higher up the Republican right's heirachy, now believed in the once-dead concept of a 'hot' Cold War, of a winnable nuclear war.

It was a frightening new government for many and even some of the Republicans' natural allies – Europe's conservatives and Christian democrats – felt more than a little uneasy. With Reagan's election in the bag both the CIA's hawks and the Latin American police states they supported decided they were now virtually untouchable. On 27 November 1980 Salvadoran security officials stood aside and deliberately allowed right-wing gunmen to kidnap 20 members of the FDR democratic opposition who'd been holding a press conference in a Jesuit high school – the mutilated bodies of six of the FDR men were dumped on the outskirts of San Salvador the next day. One of the dead victims was actually of FDR leader Enrique Alvarez Cordova.

On 2 December, after leaving San Salvador airport, four US Churchwomen 'disappeared'. The American women had long been regarded with suspicion by Salvadoran security officials who saw them as potential witnesses to state crimes...

The same day Mark Chapman boarded yet another jet plane. This time with both his .38 handgun and the deadly hollow-point ammunition – and this time he left Honolulu to fly to Chicago. Although he had a grandmother in Chicago it's extremely unlikely that the armed Chapman really spent three days and nights with her (the suspicion that he was *not* with her but involved in something far more sinister is heightened by the fact – revealed by lawyer Fenton Bresler – that the air ticket later found in Chapman's New York hotel room had been altered to make it *look* as if he flown straight to New York from Hawaii on 5 December).

On 4 December the mutilated bodies of the US churchwomen were found in a shallow unmarked grave near San Salvador's airport highway. To the American public's horror it is revealed that Ita Ford, Dorothy Kazel, Maura Clarke and Jean Donovan had all been raped and tortured before being slowly killed. Salvadoran security officials made no attempt to hide their contempt both for other death-squad victims and for the US press (before the month was out Salvadoran Treasury Police would be linked to the permanent 'disappearance' of another American citizen, reporter John Sullivan).

President Carter suspended economic and military aid to El Salvador as his Ambassador Robert E White stood by the women's graveside and thundered a warning to the murderers: 'This time they won't get away with it!' (But he was wrong: those who ordered the women's death-squad killing were never brought to justice and within weeks aid was restored to the Salvadoran regime; days later the outspoken White was dismissed by the new president, former actor Ronald Reagan. During 1981 the US would send the Salvadoran regime $30 million as it presided over the deaths of another 10,000 of its own civilians...)

That year, 1981, was when musician – and former actor – John Winston Ono Lennon would finally become eligible for full US citizenship, a citizenship which also includes the right to run for public office, to become a city mayor or even a state governor...

After at least one night in the YMCA on 63rd Street, Chapman moved into the expensive Sheraton Hotel on 7 December. He hired an upmarket call girl for the night, but despite spending $100 on getting her to his room he did not make love to her. (Chapman later explained his seemingly endless supply of money for such extravagances by saying that he had sold his Salvador Dali and Norman Rockwell paintings...but where did the 25-year-old Chapman, who never had a single well-paid job in his life, get the money to buy Rockwells and Dalis in the first place...?)

On 8 December Chapman rose early, checked his copy of *The Catcher In The Rye*, then built a little shrine of his possessions in his hotel room...

All his life, John Lennon had had a quiet obsession with the number nine – he believed it was his lucky number, luckier and more 'magical' than any other. And, whether by happenstance or destiny, the number did seem to crop up with, on and around him time and time again.

He was born at 6:30pm on 9 October 1940. Brian Epstein first saw The Beatles at the Cavern Club on 9 November 1961 and he later managed to secure The Beatles an EMI recording deal on 9 May 1962.

'She Loves You', 'Can't Buy Me Love', 'Day Tripper', 'We Can Work It Out', 'Give Peace A Chance' and 'Happy Xmas! (War Is Over)' were all singles that charted in the UK on the ninth day of the month; The Beatles created a record TV audience of 73 million in the USA on 9 February 1964 and Lennon first met Yoko Ono on 9 November, two years later.

The release of *Walls And Bridges* – with Lennon in a shirt bearing the number nine on the sleeve – came nine years after The Beatles' debut in Paris. That day, a few hours before the first French gig, John had received a neatly typed note – it contained just nine words, 'I Am Going To Shoot You At Nine Tonight...'.

Through the early evening of 8 December 1980 the Lennons continued to mix 'Walking On Thin Ice' – a stupendously powerful piece of funk-flavoured rock written, and sung, by Yoko. The plan was to issue it as a single – probably credited to Yoko – in the forthcoming New Year.

It was undoubtedly influenced by Lennon but it still made obvious – for most people for the very first time – what he had always maintained: that Ono possessed a streak of sheer musical genius. It is atmospheric, energetic *and* dramatic – nothing before or since has sounded remotely like it. From its squealing intro, through its pulsing verses, it just builds and builds, possessed of a relentless strength all its own.

Yoko's contrasting vocal is a sweetly sung narration on life and love, which is then balanced with a doomy clanking riff and her strident manic barks. Four minutes in, it reaches a plateau, the quiet in the eye of the storm, and the beat arrangement drops back a little as Ono, in confessional mode, starts to relate the story of the naive girl who tried to walk across the thin ice.

The tale ends as glacial synths surround the singer. The beat kicks back in, the track's hammer-edged riff carrying us away into a world of ruthless destiny. The shouting barks then return – it may be just the way they're recorded but the shouts sound like 'hai', the Japanese word for 'yes' – as the guitars crank up even further and chase the fade. Unsettling and emotional, to be sure, and as uneven as a mountain pass, but then Ms Ono has never wanted or claimed uniformity. It is undoubtedly a classic, brilliantly spanning both the rock and dance genres – not with ease but with a manic intensity all its own.

Curiously 'Walking On Thin Ice' also came across, even then, as if it was autobiographical, as if she somehow fully understood just how fragile life could be. But Ms Ono didn't fully understand that fragility, not then, not at that exact moment – not quite. That revelation was yet to come.

At 8:05pm photographer Paul Goresh decides to leave the sidewalk outside the Dakota. Although he's now in a unique position for a paparazzo – on speaking terms, almost friendly even, with his favourite pictorial target – he's already snapped John Lennon several times that day. The cold and hunger are also beginning to get to him and there's the drive back to New Jersey to think about as well – North Arlington just isn't that close to Manhattan.

Chapman asks him to stay a little longer, as he turns the conversation back to Lennon and the picture of him signing the *Double Fantasy* album for Chapman ('It was just a ruse,' Chapman later admits, 'I wasn't there to take his signature, I was there to take his life').

Goresh agrees to develop the film that night – Chapman offers $50 cash for a print of him with Lennon. He asks whether Goresh would think about 'shooting Lennon again' that night.

Goresh replies that he's too tired, that he can photograph Lennon almost anytime. 'But what if you never see him again?' Chapman asks abruptly and then, as Goresh walks away, he speaks up again, 'What if something happens to him…?'

In the recording studio a beaming John tells Yoko that 'Walking On Thin Ice', 'is really great, it'll be a Number One – in the disco charts at least'. Ono manages a tired smile in reply – unaware that the musical partnership that began over a dozen years before is now over. They will never record together again, for John Lennon only has minutes to live.

The Lennons leave Record Plant East at 10.30pm, telling everyone that they're going to grab a bite to eat at the Stage Deli restaurant. Six years before, on the *Rock 'n' Roll* album's cover of Lloyd Price's 'Just Because' – John's last solo recording before his 'retirement' – Lennon can be heard jokingly bidding farewell to Record Plant East. He later admitted that, even as he spoke, at the back of his mind he was actually asking himself a serious question, *is this my goodbye to the music business? Is this my goodbye…?*

In the limousine the Lennons decide to forget eating at the Stage Deli and opt to go straight home instead.

In British terms – Greenwich Mean Time – it is now well past midnight. Back in Liverpool and London it is already the ninth – December the ninth…

John and Yoko Lennon arrive back at the Dakota Building at 10:49pm Eastern Standard Time. Rather than order their driver to get them into the courtyard, the Lennons get out of the white limousine, get out on to the sidewalk. As the limo pulls away from them they walk the last few yards to the Dakota's entrance.

Mark David Chapman steps from the shadows, the loaded .38 handgun is clutched in his hand, deep in his coat pocket. Yoko walks past him, giving a tired, barely perceptible nod in answer to Chapman's blank smile, Lennon follows, a pair of cassette tapes in his eye.

Lennon's eyes meet Chapman's briefly. Neither speak. Lennon goes on walking past him. Chapman has the gun out of his pocket but it's still hidden among the folds of his coat.

Lennon is now 15 feet away. Chapman later says he hears a voice within endlessly repeating two phrases: 'I Want This! I Want This!' and 'Do It! Do It! Do It!'

Lennon is now nearly 20 feet ahead of Chapman, Yoko almost out of sight.

'Mister Lennon?'

John Lennon slows, starts to turn round as Chapman snaps into a combat pose like a hardened pro – both hands on the gun – and fires five times at Lennon. At least four shots hit Lennon in a neat cluster, the bullets slapping into his back so close together that pathologists will later have trouble marking out different entry points for each of them. A precision piece of shooting.

Once inside the victim's body, Dana Reeves' hollow points shatter in all directions with evil force, shredding Lennon's internal organs.

Yoko says later that, as the shots rang out, she thought that a 'guerrilla' war had just begun (it was a telling remark – for the peasantry of El Salvador the 'war' was already months old and their suffering would soon be replicated by fresh victims in Angola, Mozambique and Nicaragua as Reagan's backers determined to force back the clock, no matter how high the cost, no matter how bloody the task...).

To Chapman's amazement a determined Lennon somehow keeps walking, stumbling on towards the Dakota, on towards his family.

Lennon enters the Dakota. He even manages to speak, 'I'm shot, I'm shot!' He then collapses as Yoko tries to help him. With angry tears in his eyes, the ageing Dakota doorman José shakes the gun out of Chapman's hand and kicks it away. Chapman makes no effort to resist losing his only weapon. The .38 handgun skittles along the ground past John Lennon's blood-stained glasses.

'Do you know what you've done?' the doorman demands of Chapman.

'Yes,' comes the calm reply, 'I just shot John Lennon.'

José tells him to flee, 'Just get away from here!'

But after a moment of quiet reflection, Chapman merely answers the question with a question of his own.

'But where would I go?'

Chapman drops his hat and coat and casually leans against the Dakota wall. He then pulls out his latest copy of *The Catcher In The Rye*. As the seconds tick by he makes no effort to leave although two roads, a subway and Central Park all beckon. In this he stands almost unique in modern criminal history, a man who has killed a non-relative, a celebrity, and then made no attempt whatsoever to escape.

After some three and half minutes the NYPD arrive. They find a strange sight – the killer, unrestrained and still on the scene, strolling up and down as he casually reads a paperback book.

The cops handcuff him as two others carry the bloodied Lennon to their squad car, gingerly placing him in the back. Chapman looks on unconcerned – this particular 20th-century 'Chapman' has delivered his fatal message, a message from which the bloodied dream weaver before him will never recover...

One of the cops carrying Lennon mutters angry obscenities at Chapman. In a kind of reply, Chapman asks arresting officer Steven Spiro not to let anybody hurt him. After Spiro's reassurances the prisoner volunteers his first real statement to the police, a statement almost as strange as his refusal to try and escape.

'I acted alone,' Chapman says, in answer to a question that no one has even asked yet, 'I acted alone, I'm the only one...'

17 Whispers

'And when they saw him afar off, even before he came near
unto them, they conspired against him to slay him. And they said
to one another, "Behold this dreamer cometh. Come now therefore,
and let us slay him, and cast him into the pit and we will say,
'Some evil beast hath devoured him.' And then we shall see
what will become of his dreams."'
                                             – *Genesis 37.18–37.20*

'I never wanted to hurt anybody, my friends will tell you that.'
                                             – *Mark David Chapman*

Just before 11pm, Lennon arrives at Roosevelt Hospital on 9th Avenue.
Despite being diagnosed DOA – dead on arrival – the doctors try vainly
to get some response from Lennon's shattered body.

But with at least five pints of blood already lost, it's all in vain. As
with Kennedy years before, the hollow-point bullets have done their
deadly work efficiently.

At 11:15pm – according to some accounts it's nearer to 11:30pm –
Doctor Stephen Lynn and the rest of the Roosevelt's exhausted Emergency
Service Team finally give up the unequal fight.

Lennon's wife, now with label boss David Geffen, tries again to see
Lennon. This time she is told the bad news and succumbs to hysteria,
asking, 'Do you mean he's asleep? Asleep?'

As the news hits England in the morning, Roy Carr, then a senior
New Musical Express editor, takes it like a stomach punch, 'I was
speechless, lost for words for a minute. I just couldn't believe it. Neil
Spencer, he's now at *The Observer*, he was in my office at the time and

he was absolutely convinced it was a conspiracy, he kept saying so over and over again, "No way were they gonna let him come back and go on strikes and marches and stuff, no way – they killed him, didn't they? They killed him." '

At the station-house Chapman is given a strip search. Although the temperature is mild, it's found that he has on – under the fur hat, heavy-duty coat and thick full-length shirt – long johns and a thermal vest. As the night is very mild he's asked why he's so overdressed. Chapman says it's because he hates the cold, because he's from Hawaii – a comment that makes it sound as if he was a Hawaiian boy born and bred.

The NYPD's Lieutenant O'Connor then questioned Chapman. When asked the key question, of why he'd killed Lennon, Chapman gives the same reply over and over again – he just had to. John Lennon 'had' to die. John Lennon 'had' to die. *Had to.*

To O'Connor the suspect seems calm yet absent, as if he might have been 'programmed' to kill. The arresting officer Spiro, and others, are similarly impressed with Chapman's tranquil manner, especially when he takes a telephone call from his wife Gloria – only at the end of the call, after her tearful declarations of love, does Chapman show any kind of human emotion.

These unusual signs are, however, rapidly ignored. In late 1980 the NYPD was, in some ways, overwhelmed. Violent crime was edging up and tens of thousands of man-hours had been expended on the so-called 'Phantom of the Opera' killing. It was, officials later claimed, a period of desperate 'fire-fighting' – a time that was, for some, best captured in Daniel Petrie's 1981 feature film, *Fort Apache, The Bronx* starring Paul Newman, Pam Grier and Ed Asner (Asner's popular TV show *Lou Grant* was to be cancelled that same year; US sponsors including Vidal Sassoon pulled the plug after Asner dared to go on a march protesting against US support for El Salvador's death-squad government – one more sign of the growing politicisation of Reagan-era entertainment).

So the Lennon case effectively closed when Chapman signed his confessional statement less than two hours after reaching the station. The statement's version of the actual killing is backed by the Dakota Building's staff after all. A man is shot dead, someone else confesses and other witnesses pretty much back up the immediate sequence of events. End of story.

But this was the assassination of the controversial John Lennon, a world-famous superstar, a Beatle – the Beatle – now *the* male half of the (in)famous John and Yoko team, a partnership that had garnered more column inches that any other couple in recorded history (including the Reagans, the Kennedys and the royals).

Lennon's killing was a case that, at least one NYPD detective later claimed, was pursued with incredible vigour, with no detail being too small to overlook. Everything was, it was claimed, checked again and again. Yet Chapman's bizarre post-killing calm is *not* questioned, Chapman's behaviour is *not* checked with a drugs test, Chapman's 'programmed' state is *not* investigated, Chapman's previous movements are *not* thoroughly looked into, Chapman's seemingly endless cash supply is *not* analysed, nor is his time in Vietnam, nor his time in Beirut, nor his visit to China, nor his 'missing' three days in Chicago, nor why documents have been altered to cover those three days.

And when Chapman's wife refuses to be interviewed, this rejection – which can, of course, be overruled by the police in a murder case – is casually accepted. *Her husband just killed John Lennon but she doesn't want to talk? OK, fine, cool, let's just leave it at that, shall we…?*

And then there was motive. Chapman wasn't insane and he wasn't found to be insane. So why had he killed a man he'd barely met? The police knew he wasn't a serious Beatles or Lennon fan – there was only the single, day-old *Double Fantasy* album in his possession or at his house. The police also knew he wasn't a deranged autograph hunter – for a start, he didn't even own an autograph book. He wasn't a loner who killed out of 'loneliness' since he had a beautiful young wife back in Hawaii who was constantly telling him to come back home.

If Chapman was an attention seeker then why did he turn down the chance of a full trial? The 'trial of the century' as some had predicted it would be. By pleading guilty he missed all of this attention. Again, why…?

Put simply, the NYPD's investigation, or lack or it, into the John Lennon assassination was shockingly slack. With hindsight, it actually beggars belief…

The statement the NYPD took from Chapman, early on the morning of 9 December 1980, reads as follows.

'I never wanted to hurt anybody, my friends will tell you that. I have two parts in me the big part's very kind the children I've worked with will tell you that. I have a small part in me that cannot understand the big world and what goes on in it. I did not want to kill anybody and I really do not know why I did it. I fought against the small part for a long time. But for a few seconds the small part won. I asked God to help me but we are all responsible for our own actions. I have nothing against John Lennon or anything he has done in the way of music or personal beliefs. I came to New York about five weeks ago from Hawaii and the big part of me did not want to shoot John. I went back to Hawaii and tried to get rid of my small part but I couldn't. I then returned to New York on Friday 5 December 1980 I checked into the YMCA on 62nd Street I stayed one night. Then I went to the Sheraton Center 7th Avenue. Then this morning I went to the bookstore and bought *The Catcher In The Rye*. I'm sure the large part of me is Holden Caulfield who is the main person in the book. The small part of me must be the devil. I went to the building its called The Dakota. I stayed there until he came out and asked him to sign my album. At that point my big part won and I wanted to go back to my hotel, but I couldn't. I waited until he came back. He came in a car. Yoko past first and I said hello, I didn't want to hurt her. Then John came, looked at me and past me. I took the gun from my coat and pocket and fired at him. I can't believe I could do that. I just stood there clutching the book. I didn't want to run away. I don't know what happened to the gun. I just remember José kicking it away. José was crying and telling me to please leave. I felt so sorry for José. Then the police came and told me to put my hands on the wall and cuffed me.'

Signed: *Mark David Chapman*

Although the basic facts in the above 'confession' are more or less correct, with hindsight Chapman's words are most startling for what they don't say, for what they leave out.

His statement contains none of his later boasts – 'I killed the '60s!' – nor does he refer to his mind's 'little people' or his alleged hatred for John Lennon's 'phoniness'. Nor does he at any point claim to be a huge Beatles or Lennon fan.

The only possible reference to being a fan comes in the line about buying the album and getting Lennon to sign it. These are indications of being a fan, yes, but over a million people were to buy that album and dozens had it autographed. None of the others stalked the Dakota day after day with a gun.

And even this purchase of Chapman's didn't come until some three and a half weeks after *Double Fantasy* had actually been released. It was a purchase that only happened after two real Lennon fans outside The Dakota had suggested it. As Chapman himself later admitted, buying the album and getting it autographed was merely a 'ruse'.

The 'Lennon obsession', the hate for the 'phoney', his mind's 'little people', his talk of becoming a 'somebody', his smug boasts – these are all to come later, in some instances years later. They are to arrive long after the incarcerated Chapman has been in custody, long after he's taken – and made – many outside phone calls and long after he's enjoyed many extensive discussions with his various lawyers and their psychiatrists.

Even what he does say in his statement is curious enough. Apart from a seemingly obvious attempt at sketching out a schizophrenia or insanity plea for any future court case – the 'big part and the little part', the wait to be arrested – there is a strange flavour to it all. He 'never wanted to hurt' anybody, let alone John Lennon. He had, he admits, 'nothing against John Lennon' and, another curious addition this, 'I have nothing against… anything he has done in the way of music or personal *beliefs*' (our italics).

Why did Chapman stress beliefs? And why did he really kill Lennon? What made him do such a thing? And what was later to compel his wife Gloria to tell a public press conference – later screened on American TV to an audience of millions – that she was so 'sorry that John Lennon *had* to die' (our italics). Why did Lennon *have* to die?

Part of the Mark Chapman's compulsion seems to have been triggered by JD Salinger's bitter-sweet doomed-youth novel *The Catcher In The Rye*. But again, why? Why should Salinger's doomy coming-of-age novel lead to murder? Unless it was part of Chapman's programming, a trigger that could be 'fired' at him by a few simple key words. A trigger that could be 'pulled' long distance, by a cassette-tape message, by a telex, telegram or even by a telephone call. A message, or series of messages, that he could easily receive at home in Hawaii or later in a hotel room – or even later, under arrest in a police cell.

If, as increasingly seems the case, Chapman was a programmed killer – like Sirhan Sirhan – then it appears that his programmers had learnt something since Sirhan 'assassinated' RFK.

Sirhan had post-killing chills despite the blistering heat of LA that June of 1968 – chills are one sign of deep hypnosis, a sign Sirhan repeated when he was hypnotised in his cell by Dr Diamond. These chills were noticed and they helped feed the 'programmed Sirhan' theory (a theory that looks more and more like fact as time passes).

When Chapman was arrested this problem was overcome, despite the mildness of the weather – it was over 45 degrees Fahrenheit in New York on the evening of 8 December 1980 – he had on a heavy shirt, equally heavy trousers, a full thick overcoat, a fur hat plus thermal long johns with a thermal vest. No wonder Chapman didn't replicate Sirhan's chills that night. When he was asked why he was so heavily dressed, Chapman told the NYPD it was because he was 'from' tropical Hawaii. But he wasn't 'from' Hawaii, he'd just lived there for a few years. He was, in fact, born and raised in continental USA.

Then there was the Beirut incident – why had a serious, committed Christian gone to the Middle East yet avoided the holy places? It was a strange anomaly that someone must have noticed – perhaps one of Chapman's intelligence 'handlers' – for it was dealt with some three years later. At the very end of his 1978 world tour Chapman squeezed in a couple of days in Israel and there he gave a couple of the holy sites a cursory visit.

It was nothing to the weeks he'd just spent elsewhere – in India and Thailand, for instance – but it did make up for his earlier 'oversight' and now that box could be ticked off. Holy sites – not avoided. Been there, done that.

If anyone ever asked Chapman he could now honestly say he had visited some of the Christian shrines during his time in the Middle East...

And, almost certainly unlike Sirhan, Chapman *did* fire the gun that killed Lennon. The MK/ULTRA programme seemed to have advanced to the point where the 'fall guy' no longer had to just be on the scene – like Oswald – while other professionals did the real job. Nor did he merely – like Sirhan – have to fire off blank after noisy blank while the real killers discreetly did their work.

No, in all probability Chapman was the real thing – the first real, known Manchurian Candidate. In that context Lennon's assassination actually makes *more* sense, not less. Of course Lennon was important and of course his resurgent rock career and returning street activism would have embarrassed the incoming Reagan regime.

Yet even then, the killing of a musician – even a famous man of the Left – seems to be a remarkably paranoid act if it serves no other purpose. If it is seen, and ordered, in total isolation. But add to that the growing hysteria of the US Right during 1979–80 and then – even more importantly – add the final fulfilment of the CIA's secretly continued MK/ULTRA programme and you have another, stronger rationale.

Think about it just for a moment. With one stroke an annoyingly popular, radical irritant has been removed, just when he needs to be, *and also* – at last – the 'automatic gunman' project that's been running, on and off, for some 30 years has finally, successfully, been tested. You have a patsy who actually *does* kill for you – rather than just muddy the waters – a fall-guy who murders then calmly accepts the consequences for actions that are not his own (and if any blame does trickle down then – as with Oswald, Ray and Sirhan – there are the various Phase One, Two and Three fullbacks, 'lone nut', 'stalker', 'schizo fan', which many media pundits will happily peddle till the cows come home).

Of course, professional hypnotists have usually maintained that no one can be made to do things under hypnosis that they would not normally do in real life. Yet, while there is a grain of truth in this, it does not apply to everyone. It does not apply to those who already have a mildly disturbed background or those especially susceptible to hypnosis – or those who have been simultaneously treated with drugs (to induce, say, model psychosis).

Nor does it apply to those hypnosis subjects who have also been paid large sums of cash – and promised even more – to voluntarily undergo such treatment as part of a special 'patriotic mission'. Under deep hypnosis, blocks can be introduced – the subject can remember absolutely nothing, not even when asked to recall such things under 'normal' hypnosis. To get at the truth can then take years of follow-up sessions, as well as complete cooperation.

Oswald underwent hypnosis so he wouldn't give away more secrets than he was supposed to – nothing beyond the U-2 spy plane – when interrogated by the Soviets in 1959–61.

Sirhan underwent this so he could complete his 'secret mission' and gain the $80,000 he continually wrote about in his diaries (even adding the cover-up words, 'I have never heard "please pay to the order of of of of..." this or that 80,000...' [our italics]); and it was Sirhan who answered all questions instantaneously under hypnosis in custody – all, that is, except questions about if he'd really killed RFK alone or if there had been any kind of conspiracy behind the death – and then his answers were delayed for between three to five seconds, significant pauses in such circumstances.

Chapman underwent his hypnosis so he could fulfil the 'special training' that had taken him round the world, principally into danger areas like Vietnam, Beirut and Red China. Training that was to give him money and prepare him for his ultimate action, action that was to be triggered by a simple phrase – or a line from a book (like, say, *The Catcher In The Rye*).

At some point his handlers had been forced to let him know he stood a good chance of getting caught. But his training had prepared him for this eventuality. For his training included observing the treatment he got following his fake unwitnessed 'suicide' attempt in Hawaii – and the subsequent months he spent actually working in the same psychiatric wing of Hawaii's Castle Medical Center, observing the patients. This was all perfect preparation for 'acting up' enough to cop an insanity plea and stroll out of a mental hospital just a couple of years later, a leaner, freer and richer man.

Of course, he'd have to change his identity in order to avoid revenge attacks by Beatle and Lennon fans but – his handlers no doubted assured him – if Mob informers and crime witnesses could be given a new identity then so could Chapman once he'd spent a year or two being analysed. And it all almost worked – several of the psychiatrists who analysed Chapman before sentencing talked about 'schizophrenia' and 'mental disturbance', he was halfway to a successful 'insanity plea'.

The 'breakdown' Chapman underwent before sentencing was possibly genuine, at least in part – for there's a big difference between getting 20 months in hospital and 20 years to life in a maximum-security prison. Some things can't be prepared for, not 100 per cent (but, even here, during his breakdown, a berserk Chapman climbed the high bars of his cell like a monkey, something that Sirhan had done a dozen years before – when under Dr Diamond's hypnosis…).

Even if one wishes to disregard all of the above there *are* factual cases of hypnosis being used to commit crime by proxy. In Denmark in 1951, hypnotist Bjorn Nielsen put Palle Handrup into a deep trance and ordered him to rob a Copenhagen bank and shoot dead anyone who tried to stop him. The crime was carried out and after Nielsen had grabbed the cash a bemused Handrup was rapidly jailed – however, in prison Handrup began to recall details about Nielsen and the final hypnosis session. There were, however, still some 'blocks' on what he could recall.

A psychiatrist with experience of hypnotic technique finally got the full story after 11 months of 'unblocking' Handrup, who was eventually pardoned and freed.

In April 1994, Mexican presidential candidate Colosio was assassinated apparently by 'lone nut' assassin Aburto. The latter said he had 'no intention' whatsoever of killing Colosio until the candidate came close and a voice within ordered him to shoot Colosio's feet.

The local Chief of Police did not believe Aburto had acted of his own free will – nor did he believe that Aburto was the only gunman that day. The policeman's investigation came to an abrupt halt, however, when 'persons unknown' shot and killed him.

The Mexico government's official inquiry concluded that Colosio had been assassinated – probably with the help of 'mind control' experts – a killing carried out by well-supported conspirators whom the Mexican police have been unable to trace.

And then there are these quotes – all by men found *sane* by the legal system, all of them talking with respect and even affection about the men they assassinated.

'I'm not a malcontent,
nothing irritated me about the President [Kennedy].'
Lee Harvey Oswald
speaking after he'd allegedly assassinated JFK

'I liked [Robert] Kennedy,
he stood up for the little guy.'
Sirhan Sirhan
speaking after he'd allegedly assassinated RFK

'I didn't mean to hurt anybody...
I like John Lennon.'
Mark David Chapman
speaking after Lennon's assassination

There is one final point on hypnosis, or mesmerism as it was once known. Despite so many people proclaiming it to be 'just harmless fun' without any dangerous applications, the fact remains that no major television network anywhere in the world will ever permit a 'to camera' broadcast of a full hypnosis session...

On 20 January 1981 Ronald Reagan was inaugurated as President of the USA. Within hours word came from Iran revealing that, after 444 days, the American hostages had suddenly been released and put on a plane west. On hearing the news, the recently defeated Carter and his VP Walter 'Fritz' Mondale both broke down and wept.

Five years later – with Republican activists trying to get the US Constitution's 'Roosevelt amendment' changed so the still-popular Reagan could run for a third term – his government was abruptly shaken by the Irangate-Contragate revelations – namely that the US had been selling arms to Revolutionary Iran and then using the cash to illegally fund Nicaragua's right-wing Contra terrorists. The prime mover in the Irangate affair was National Security Council adviser Colonel Oliver North (the born-again Christian who helped get an acquittal for Randy Herrod, patrol leader during the 1970 Southang massacre in South Vietnam). In the fall-out from the Irangate-Contragate scandal, Oliver North was forced to resign from the NSC and all talk of Reagan being allowed a third presidential term was quietly dropped…

18 Connections

'We can use the available political machinery to screw
our political enemies!'
– *John Dean, legal counsel to President Nixon, August 1971*

It's a mainstream commonplace that the assassinations of JFK,
Malcolm X, MLK, RFK and John Lennon are all far too 'big' to have
official involvement. How can it be true? How could they possibly dare?

Yet, the big lie has a long-running, if dishonourable, history, in every
corner of this, our beleaguered planet. If the lie's big enough then, as the
Nazis secretly proclaimed, people will believe it. And it was the Nazis'
own SS killers that time and again told their victims, as millions were
beaten and murdered all around them, 'It doesn't matter if you alone
somehow manage to survive all this, it won't matter for no one will ever
believe this ever happened anyway, no one will ever believe you…'.

This evil cry has had many echoes down the years – echoed by
Rwanda's genocidal Hutu killers, by Pol Pot's Khmer Rouge torturers,
by El Salvador's Army and its death squads, by Milosevic's concentration
camp guards. *No one will believe you.*

And thousands, perhaps millions, do not believe the victims. There
are still those who insist that most of the above holocausts or massacres
did *not* happen or were, at worst, a small aberration, on a tiny scale.

Such duplicity had always lurked within people, and those of
intelligence have always recognised this fact. The day in April 1945, for
instance, that the Nazi camp at Bergen Belsen was liberated, a British
officer present insisted that one of his men write down the names of every
soldier there – when asked why, he replied it was because one day someone
would deny that such a crime had ever been committed.

Richard Dimbleby recorded a radio programme about the same camp but the BBC refused to believe his account about tens of thousands of civilian inmates being starved and murdered. They subsequently refused to broadcast it. Eventually Dimbleby Senior had to threaten to resign before the corporation reluctantly broadcast what he, and hundreds of others, had witnessed with their own eyes.

Photographs? Witnesses? Memos? Reams of circumstantial evidence? Full confessions even? Not good enough. To some it doesn't matter how much proof is ever offered. For their own emotional or financial reasons they will deny the evidence of everything, even the evidence of their own ears and eyes. *No one will believe you.*

When a genuine madman, a real 'lone nut' – or an untrained member of the public – attempts an assassination, the botched hallmarks are obvious. When several of Charles Manson's gun groupies attempted to kill President Ford the bullets missed by miles.

When John Hinckley tried to assassinate President Reagan he caused only a temporary injury to the president. When Michael Abram tried to murder George Harrison on 30 December 1999, Harrison was hurt but not killed. When the professionals – like elements within the CIA or their proxies – hit an individual they stay hit. Dead. Period. The fact that the CIA can utilise the FBI, the DIA, the DEA and US Naval Intelligence can only make committing such crimes easier. The fact that local American police forces, much of the legal establishment and even some sections of the media can then be pressurised into quickly accepting the official verdict can only make 'covering up' much easier.

No one's perfect, of course, and mistakes do lead to clues, which can slip out. And connections between apparently unrelated people do, after a time, slowly slip to the surface.

So then, what are the connections between the Nixon Mob, the FBI and the assassinations? And what of the assassins of John F Kennedy, Robert F Kennedy, Martin Luther King and John Lennon? Are there really more than one or two faint links between Lee Harvey Oswald, James Earl Ray, Sirhan Bishara Sirhan and Mark David Chapman?

Below is a brief rundown of the similarities, the 'startling coincidences', that seem to draw together the 'big shots' and the killers of those who happened to speak out against them and their wars. It is not a definitive list by any means, respected American assassination experts such as James DiEugenio, Lisa Pease and Mark Lane could – if they wished – produce even more links. But the following does give a flavour of what has slowly become public knowledge, some of it over the last year or two.

Connections – The Illicit Establishment

Richard Nixon, Jack Ruby, E Howard Hunt, Bernard Barker and Frank Sturgis all supported or worked with red-baiter Senator Joe McCarthy in the '50s.

- Nixon employed Ruby, Hunt, Barker and Sturgis during his political career.
- Nixon, Ruby, Hunt, Barker and Sturgis all worked on the failed 1960 invasion of Cuba, the Bay of Pigs fiasco.
- Nixon, Ruby, Hunt, Barker and Sturgis all worked with the CIA – Nixon working with them for years as Vice President.
- Nixon, Ruby, Hunt, Barker and Sturgis all worked in the American Deep South.
- Nixon, Ruby, Hunt, Barker and Sturgis were all present in Dallas on 22 November 1963 when JFK was assassinated – Barker has been identified by police officer Seymour Weitzman as being the so-called 'Secret Service agent' who prevented policemen and others from inspecting the grassy knoll in the seconds after the JFK shooting while Hunt once went to court to try and prevent his presence in Dallas that day becoming public knowledge.
- Nixon, Ruby, Hunt, Barker and Sturgis are all later suspected of being involved in, or at the very least aware of, the plot to assassinate JFK.
- Hunt and Sturgis, as gunmen, have long been actual assassination suspects.
- Nixon, Hunt, Sturgis, Barker and Liddy all discussed the 'John Lennon case'.
- Nixon and Hoover both had Lennon tailed and wire-tapped.

- Nixon, Hunt, Sturgis and Barker were all aware of the 1972 Watergate burglary.
- Hunt, Sturgis and Barker were all prosecuted over the 1972 Watergate burglary – Barker was actually the leader of the Watergate break-in team and was later jailed.
- Nixon, Ruby, Hunt, Barker and Sturgis all finally came to grief over their involvement with the Watergate break-in.

Nixon, after stalling for over two years, was finally forced to resign his presidency on 8 August 1974. During Nixon's active political career hundreds of virtual innocents had been ruined by his work with McCarthy while President Kennedy, Malcolm X, Martin Luther King and Robert F Kennedy had all later been assassinated.

During his presidency the Governor of Alabama had been badly wounded in an assassination attempt, the democratically elected government of Chile had been violently overthrown and at least 25,000 American troops – plus over one million native civilians – had died in Vietnam.

Nixon, who'd been in charge of overseeing the CIA during his time as VP, had accumulated plenty of enemies – people who, with some justification, wanted their day in court as well as some recompense for the very real losses they had suffered. People who wanted to know why, and for how long, he'd employed Jack Ruby. People who wanted to know what words had been edited out of the so-called 'Watergate tapes'.

Within a month of Nixon's resignation, however, the new Republican president – ex-Warren Commissioner Gerald Ford – enraged commentators by giving Richard Nixon a full pardon. This presidential pardon effectively freed 'Tricky Dicky' Nixon from the possibility of ever being prosecuted or jailed for any of his long list of indiscretions – it also saved him from having to answer any questions about the legal, and illegal, activities of both Hoover's FBI and the CIA...

Connections – The Alleged Assassins

Lee Harvey Oswald, James Earl Ray and Mark David Chapman were all painted as loners yet all of them had partners, lovers or wives as well as friends.

- Oswald, Sirhan Sirhan, Ray and Chapman all left damaging clues against themselves despite all being of average or above average intelligence (clues included writings and the public/mail-order purchase of guns and bullets that could have been bought anonymously).
- Oswald, Sirhan and Chapman all consorted with religious extremists of the Christian far right (the 1976 Church Committee forced an admission from the CIA that the Agency had over 20 Christian 'missionaries' on its payroll – along with over 40 agents who liaised with local police forces in New York, LA and other US cities).
- Oswald, Sirhan and Chapman all showed confused or homosexual tendencies.
- Oswald, Ruby and JFK assassination suspect Ferrie were described as 'bedmates' by many witnesses.
- Oswald, Sirhan and Chapman all had Middle Eastern connections – all centred around Iran or Beirut, the latter being a centre of US Naval Intelligence operations throughout the '60s and '70s as well as being the alleged site of an assassination training camp.
- Oswald, Sirhan and Chapman all travelled extensively despite being, ostensibly, penniless.
- Oswald, Ray, Sirhan and Chapman all made blatantly crass and public anti-American statements which they obviously did not believe (Oswald's insulting of US cars and ridiculous praising of their Soviet equivalents, Ray's attack on America's tolerance of blacks, Sirhan's declarations of war against a 'corrupt' America, Chapman's laughter at the Pearl Harbor memorial ceremonies).
- Oswald and Chapman, despite public gestures to the contrary, were both heavily against Castro's Cuba.
- Oswald, Sirhan and Chapman all showed classic signs of being hypnotised and/or programmed.

- Oswald, Sirhan and Chapman were all described as being enormously 'calm' after the assassinations.
- Oswald and Sirhan both spoke several languages, including Russian – a language Chapman also attempted to learn.
- Oswald and Sirhan both had their incredible 'marksmanship' officially explained by 'magic bullets' (Oswald apparently used one, Sirhan three…).
- Oswald, Ruby and Chapman all visited YMCA centres even when they had the money for hotels and/or companionship (and Chapman, seven years after being jailed, was still writing to YMCA directors).
- Oswald and Ruby both had contacts, with both the FBI and CIA.
- Oswald and Ruby both had their own files with both the FBI and CIA.
- Oswald, Sirhan and Chapman were all the subjects of official documentation that has been either altered or destroyed (Oswald's CIA and FBI files are much deleted while his US Army file was destroyed in 1973, Sirhan's gun forensic files are both inaccurate and incomplete, while Chapman's YMCA file is missing and his crucial 5 December 1980 flight ticket had been altered).
- Oswald and Chapman were both amongst the very first US citizens to visit communist nations (Oswald with his short-lived defection to the USSR in 1959, Chapman with his visits to Vietnam and China in 1978).
- Oswald and Chapman both made 'suspicious' suicide attempts. The latter's was not seen by anybody, while Oswald's was not taken seriously at all.
- Oswald, Sirhan, Ray and Chapman despite all being described as 'lone nuts', 'schizophrenics' and the like, were all found to be sane at the time of their arrest.
- Oswald, Sirhan, Ray and Chapman despite all being described as being 'lone nuts', 'schizophrenics' and the like,were all found to be sane at the time of their arraignment.
- Sirhan, Ray and Chapman were all found sane by the courts.
- Sirhan, Ray and Chapman, despite being labelled attention-seekers, all rejected the chance of a full public trial by pleading guilty.
- Sirhan and Chapman both chanted, or wrote, repetitiously before the assassinations – another classic sign of programming (Sirhan scribbling 'RFK Must Die! RFK Must Die! RFK Must Die!' – this was written

days before RFK publicly agreed with the sale of US jets to Israel, which Sirhan's defence lawyers claimed was the real motive for the RFK killing – while Chapman chanted, 'The Phony Must Die Says The Catcher In The Rye! John Lennon Must Die Says The Catcher In The Rye...').

- Sirhan and Chapman both climbed the bars of their cells like monkeys, Sirhan after being ordered to do so in a hypnosis session and Chapman during one of his post-guilty plea 'breakdowns' (Dr Eduard Simson-Kallas, San Quentin prison's chief psychologist, observed Sirhan over many hours and to this day is certain that the prisoner had indeed been 'hypnoprogrammed').
- Sirhan and Chapman both wrote, 'please pay to the order of...' over and over again.
- Oswald was shot dead before his trial but Ray died in a 'normal' prison for the sane.
- Sirhan and Chapman both made clumsy attempts to be appear insane but only after heavy prison sentences loomed.
- Sirhan and Chapman both today remain in 'normal' prisons for the sane...

...WIRE STORY: ...WEDNESDAY 27 SEPTEMBER 2000...LENNON ASSASSIN TRIES FOR PAROLE

The one-time Hawaiian resident Mark David Chapman who assassinated former Beatle John Lennon in 1980 will get his first parole hearing this coming Tues. (Oct 3rd). Chapman, currently serving 20 years to life at Attica Correctional Facility, Rochester, NY, worked with psychiatrists at the Castle Medical hospital in late 1977 thru' to 1979 before transferring to Castle's community relations unit.

He shot dead Lennon in NYC on December 8th 1980. Chapman speaking for the first time in nine years claimed that Lennon himself would probably want him freed.

Chapman has been reported for some small-scale infractions while in Attica though he has since obtained work in the law library. He now says he feels some remorse for the Lennon slaying. It was, he said, 'terrible' that Lennon was dead.

Eliot Mintz, a spokesman for Lennon's widow Yoko Ono, said that she had sent a letter to the parole board but did not disclose the letter's contents

...WIRE STORY ENDS...

...WIRE STORY: ...CHAPMAN UPDATE 4 OCTOBER 2000 – CHAPMAN, MAN WHO KILLED JOHN LENNON, DENIED PAROLE...

No further details yet available on parole failure of Mark David Chapman – now claiming, for the third time, to have discovered God – after Oct 3rd parole hearing. Chapman shot John Lennon Dec 8th 1980 and avoided trial by pleading guilty

...WIRE STORY ENDS...

...WIRE STORY: ...26 JUNE 2003 ...SIRHAN SIRHAN ATTORNEY DEMANDS RFK ASSASSINATION RETRIAL...

Thirty five years after RFK's assassination, Lawrence Teeter, Sirhan Sirhan's lawyer, has forcefully argued that his client had been hypnoprogrammed and thus framed for the killing, possibly by a conspiracy set up by elements of the [US] government.

'The guy was set up, he remembers nothing whatsoever of the shooting,' Teeter told reporters, 'there is an innocent man sitting in prison...'

Sirhan is currently serving a life sentence in Corcoran State Prison after eventually pleading guilty to assassinating Senator Bobby Kennedy – then a 42-year-old presidential candidate – in LA in June 1968.

He has since been denied parole a dozen times – lastly in March 2002 – and Teeter now wants the whole case moved from LA to Fresno since one of those who originally prosecuted Sirhan has since become a federal judge in the LA area thus making, in Teeter's eyes, a free and fair trial impossible.

'Those who wanted Robert Kennedy killed were those who were not satisfied with his promise to end the Vietnam War,' said

Teeter who believes the 'military-industrial complex' is to blame. He maintains that Sirhan Sirhan was hypnotised into firing shots at RFK and that Sirhan was almost certainly using blanks rather than the real, fatal, bullets.

Either way Sirhan could not have fired the actual shot that killed Robert Kennedy since all the witnesses put him at least two feet away from Kennedy. RFK's fatal wound was fired in from less than two inches. The case's coroner Thomas Noguchi even admitted this at the time and has not denied it since. Sirhan's original defense team were only informed of this 'one inch – two feet' discrepancy once the original trial had already begun. The original jury were never told about it.

Also Teeter believes that prosecutors blackmailed Sirhan's original defense attorney into 'throwing the case' and that police and government intelligence agencies conducted the assassination investigation inadequately, disregarding and browbeating many key witnesses and ignoring the other men who were seen with guns around the scene of the crime that night (June 4th–5th 1968). This was done, Teeter and his team believe, purely in order to produce a 'whitewash' verdict.

Although she has not, at time of writing, answered any of Teeter's specific points, LA County DA Sandi Gibbons, who covered the first Sirhan Sirhan trial as a junior reporter, said, 'I don't think so, no. I think that the person who shot and killed Robert Kennedy was convicted and sentenced properly. Absolutely. And after a fair trial too…I think Sirhan killed him [RFK]. And he killed him alone.'

Teeter is petitioning an LA federal court for a full public retrial. 'The integrity of the [American] judicial process is at stake here,' he said…

…RFK–SIRHAN 26/6/03…

…WIRE STORY ENDS…

19 Not Fade Away

'The mass of men serve the State thus, not as men mainly, but as machines, with their bodies. They are the standing army, and the militia, jailers, constables, posse comitatus etc – in most cases there is no exercise whatever of the judgment or of the moral sense; they put themselves on a level with wood and earth and stones; and wooden men can perhaps be manufactured that will serve their purposes as well. Such command no more respect than men of straw, such should command no more respect than a lump of dirt...yet such as these even are commonly esteemed good citizens. Others – as most legislators, politicians, lawyers, ministers and office-holders – serve the State chiefly with their heads; and, as they rarely make any moral distinctions, they are as likely to serve the Devil, without intending to, as God.

A very few, as heroes, patriots, martyrs, reformers in the great sense, and men, serve the State with their consciences also, and so necessarily resist it for the most part; and they are commonly treated as enemies by it.'

– *Henry David Thoreau*, Civil Disobedience

'John took the [FBI] battle seriously, but he had great trust in... the American justice system. I think he always knew it would turn out fine.'

– *May Pang*

Jon Wiener's quest, to free *all* of the John Lennon FBI files, seemed to have reached a dead end by the summer of 1997, stuck on the problem of the files pertaining to a foreign power – that is, Britain. But the election of a new Labour government, ending 18 years of Tory rule, promised change. The incoming prime minister, Tony Blair, headed an administration pledged to achieving an unparalleled 'openness in government'.

There was even to be a new law, which would replace the selective 30-year rule that had obtained in the UK since the '70s. Finally, after centuries of obstruction, the British were to be allowed some kind of freedom of information act.

The renegade MI5 spy David Shayler gave his employers a nudge by revealing the fact that there were British files on Lennon – over his support for left-wing parties – as well as on two '60s students who were now members of the new cabinet (these were former student union leader Jack Straw and one-time anti-apartheid activist Peter Hain).

Weeks later MI5 began to shred over 120,000 of the files it had held on UK subjects – including one John Winston Ono Lennon. Rather than fight this outrageous action, the government actually seemed to encourage it – perhaps grateful that the youthful excesses of its senior and junior ministers would now never be made public. Those who'd been less successful in life than high-ranking government members – those who might have had their careers slowed or even destroyed by secret action – were the losers. They would not be able to claim compensation without proof. And that proof was rapidly being turned into pulp beside the south bank of the Thames.

But the US copies of the MI5 Lennon files – or at least those that were sent to the FBI – did still exist. And after much prompting from Wiener and his civil-liberties legal team, the FBI agreed to ask for British permission to finally release the last ten Lennon documents – those FBI files that had originated in, contained information from – or were copied to – Military Intelligence 5 and 6.

Yet, despite all their freedom of information pledges, Blair's regime hesitated for a few days, and then said 'no'. Lennon's 'All You Need Is Love' might have been good enough for the government's Millennium Dome party VIP singalong – and the Queen's Golden Jubilee celebrations – but the remaining FBI files on him were to remain secret, if Downing Street and Whitehall were to have anything at all to do with it. But why have successive British governments gone to all this trouble, this decades' long trail of obstruction? Why has the Blair administration – already on the rack over PR 'spin' and unfulfilled election promises – effectively given up on open government, giving their critics yet another stick to beat them with?

What are Blair and company protecting? The fact that a few youthful indiscretions, much censored, might slip out? They cannot be worried about revealing the names of former radical, or showbiz, informers since those specific names would be blanked out anyway. What really concerns them? That the files might reveal that – under the successive Wilson, Heath and Thatcher regimes – there was a level of surveillance here to match that of the Stasi? Or could it possibly be something even more sinister? Were MI5, and possibly MI6, passing on UK approval for foreign, that is, FBI and CIA, surveillance of a UK citizen, one John Winston Ono Lennon? Or perhaps it was even worse. Maybe it was British intelligence and/or the government giving permission to deport Lennon? Or even permission to kill him…?

It all sounds so over the top, so far-fetched – even an all-American assassination – and yet…John Lennon *is* dead, JFK, MLK and RFK *were* all assassinated, the official inquiries *were* worthless, the Watergate, Contragate and Irangate scandals did happen, their conspirators were caught and the FBI *did* fight a 16-year court battle to try and prevent most of their 281 pages on Lennon ever being seen (and even now, despite America's Freedom of Information act, 13 of the pages since released are effectively unreadable).

And since Lennon's death MI5 and the Thatcher, Major and Blair administrations *have* all taken their turn to sit on the dustbins, *have* all taken their turn at keeping the rest of us in the dark…

As a British citizen I now find it almost embarrassing that, Fenton Bresler aside, time and time again it has been Americans – principally Jon Wiener, Dan Marmalefsky and Mark Rosenbaum – whose actions have put most pressure on the FBI – and thus on MI5 and the UK government – to reveal the truth about the persecution of John Lennon. A truth still not yet fully told.

John Lennon was a British citizen by birth and he spent the first 31 years of his life here. During his time here he employed dozens of people directly and thousands indirectly. He paid millions of pounds in taxes to Britain and helped generate millions more. He gave hundreds of thousands in cash to charities, anti-war organisations and popular causes, most of them honourable.

For his services to the British music industry he was awarded the Order of the British Empire and though he returned the accompanying medal – in protest over the slaughter in Biafra and Vietnam – it is an honorary award, which still stands. When he died he was officially still John Winston Ono Lennon OBE...

Perhaps one day Blair and his Downing Street 'First Lady' could stop singing Beatles' songs long enough to ask why their government still prevents full FBI disclosure of the first Beatle's files. Perhaps one day someone, somewhere within Britain's bloated establishment should 'give a damn' about all this...

Summer 2003. Sales of Beatles recordings now exceed one billion. If cover versions, bootlegs and solo recordings by John Lennon and the others are included then the figure rises to nearly two billion – *two thousand million discs*. More recording copies than there are families on planet earth. Well over 100 million of these have been bought since Lennon's death...

A single one of the 60 cut-outs from the *Sergeant Pepper* cover was auctioned at Christie's in London, the five-foot piece of cardboard realized over £86,000 ($130,000)...

At any moment, at literally any time of the day or night, at least three Lennon-McCartney songs are being played on radio stations somewhere in the world...

What would once have been considered laughable is now plain fact – it is a certainty that the work recorded by John Lennon, with both The Beatles and Yoko Ono, will continue to be played – and enjoyed and covered – as long as music is played. He, with their help, turned a fading musical fad into the biggest cultural force of the 20th century – obligatory for every advert, movie, TV show, club, party and gathering. The soundtrack of an entire globe.

Where would John Lennon be now, in this post-Cold War world, this globalised, multicultural, designer world? A planet that now has mobile video phones, the World Wide Web and credit-card sized computers – as well as 800 million citizens still going hungry. If anyone wrote 'Imagine' today, it would surely be with different lyrics ('below us only GM crops, above us Murdoch's Sky (™…')

Musically it's easy to imagine Lennon warming to the dance and technology explosions of the '80s and early '90s – he had, after all, helped break soul music in both Britain and in the US in the '60s and he was always interested in studio technology – though he would perhaps have become concerned at the growing number of musicians being prematurely thrown on the scrap heap (and at the growing number of 'new' tracks that are simply sampled rip-offs of older songs).

Britpop and the various indie revivals would no doubt have raised a wry, appreciative smile – new wave of new wave of new wave, anyone? – as would the music, and antics, of Oasis and other such groups.

It's pretty certain too he'd still be standing for peace, though he'd be suspicious of any 'peace' that merely meant the killing went on, out of sight, in the torture chambers of dictators. Similarly he'd still be promoting racial and sexual equality though he'd probably be too streetwise to wholly embrace the political correctness mentality and its blend of reverse racism and endless hypocritical hierarchies.

His – and Yoko's – love of nature and organic food suggest he'd now be at the forefront of those protesting against deforestation and the dangers of GM 'Frankenstein' food – as well as the ruthless globalisation of the world economy with which such phenomena are inextricably linked…

And yet, even the most carefully weighed speculation, while fascinating, is, in the end, wrong-headed. At least in all the ways that really count. Such speculation starts off from the wrong point like, say, Robert Harris's otherwise brilliant 'what if' novel *Fatherland*, which had Beatles songs being played across a Nazi-occupied Britain (as if Hitler's brutal culture police could possibly have nurtured Merseybeat in the same distant way that Atlee and Churchill inadvertently did).

You cannot just plonk John Lennon down at the start of this 21st century. If he had been alive all along throughout the '80s and '90s – if he had not been killed – then things, no matter how small the change, would be different now. It was Lennon, after all, who'd sung about wanting to change the world and it was not a line delivered from a position of total inexperience, it was something he'd already done once before.

Lennon's fame and wealth – and *conscience* – could, and undoubtedly would, have been used again to support the causes close to his heart. His physical presence added tens of thousands to demonstrations and his words brought global media attention.

In the words of one of his few journalistic friends, ex-musician Roy Carr, 'John could connect with the disenfranchised, the guy in the street, he could speak in terms that they understood – when he wanted to. And people *did* listen to him. When you've got the ears of that many people and you're not in government, or a government-sponsored opposition, then you're a threat, to them you're a real threat' (today, Carr – like Sean Lennon, Fenton Bresler and many others – now suspects that US intelligence had something to do with Lennon's death and/or the subsequent cover-up).

This political 'threat' of which Carr speaks is the real reason Lennon was placed under FBI surveillance in the first place – in Wiener's memorable phrase, the start of a sort of 'rock 'n' roll Watergate'. Because of John Lennon's opposition to the war in Vietnam he was a potential 'threat'. An enemy of the war mongers.

And when the 'new Vietnam' began – with the US backing the death-squad governments then ruling most of Central America – Lennon's comeback made him a threat once more. The first Vietnam ended in defeat and the disgrace of Watergate, the second ended in a bloody armistice and the equally disgraceful Contragate affair.

But by then such events could not hold up the general movement towards the Right's spectacular Cold War triumph over Gorbachev's 'evil empire'. Of course, in order to 'win', the West in general – and the US intelligence services in particular – had to arm and encourage some pretty nasty people, from Salvadoran death squads to Burmese heroin dealers, to the Taliban and Bin Laden factions in Afghanistan. The latter killed and tortured thousands, most of them innocents, and even started schools of terrorism and bigotry to brutalise the next generation as the funds continued to roll in from across the Atlantic. But such gruesome 'side-effects' didn't matter as far as the experts in Langley and Washington were concerned – the fanatical killers would surely stop when they were asked to. Wouldn't they…?

Yet the free-market 'Coca-Cola victory' that has resulted is actually one that's left the West's citizens more stressed, insecure and overworked than ever, a victory that's left their schools, hospitals and streets more dirty and dangerous than they've been in living memory, a victory that's left their borders besieged and their future uncertain, a victory that's now made it impossible for them to travel safely anywhere in Africa, Asia, the Middle East or Latin America, a victory that's left them vulnerable almost everywhere, unsafe even in the air-conditioned skyscrapers of Lower Manhattan… In the past generals who delivered such 'victories' have faced outrage and court-martial…

There were, of course, millions of victims before the Cold War was 'won'. But few of them were musicians and fewer still were world famous – only one was John Winston Ono Lennon, ex-Beatle, poet, composer, peace activist.

It now seems obvious that his death was actually *not* – as many commentators have blithely concluded – the first fatal celebrity stalking. It was instead, almost certainly the first completely successful MK/ULTRA killing – 'delivered' without lookalikes or large-scale back-up by an assassin so deeply 'programmed' that even now, decades on, he still has no idea why he committed one of the most shocking crimes of the late 20th century (an attitude that ensures his continuing imprisonment).

In that sense, Lennon's killing was the last of the '60s assassinations. For all their faults, the Kennedys, Martin Luther King and even, in the last months of his life, Malcolm X, had all stood for brotherhood, for the possibility of positive change, for the belief that love was stronger than hate and that, ultimately, people were more important than money.

It was something that John Lennon, for all his indulgences, also believed in. It was something that the first post-'50s decade had, for all its extremes, rapidly come to stand for. And so the target that dark December night was thus John Lennon himself, at the height of his comeback. For he was the man who symbolised, more than anyone else, The Beatles, the band that, more than any other band, was the '60s – those ten tumultuous years that the right-wing Tory Norman Tebbit once called 'that cheap, overrated decade', the ten years that most other people remember as the 'the last real decade of hope'...

As these words are being written, John is back in the headlines again – 'Did Lennon Bed ALL The Beatle Wives?', 'Did John Lennon Really Kill The Fifth Beatle?' – as acquaintances continue, wittingly or unwittingly, the hatchet job that author Albert Goldman began some 20 years ago.

Friends once again had to issue the same denials – no, John had not killed May Pang or tried to kill Yoko Ono, nor had he slept with all his band's spouses and, no, nor had he murdered his old friend Stuart Sutcliffe.

A constant smearing of the memory is something that the Lennons, like the Kennedys, have had to get used to. Nowadays, if one talks of a US leader who had dozens of lovers, who spied on his friends for the FBI, who encouraged an abortion, who indulged in multiple adultery, who's been accused of 'date rape', who will we all think of? JFK, of course. But, as recent revelations show, the above is actually the case record of another president, one Ronald Reagan.

Other lies or exaggerations about JFK remain in circulation – principally that he was a Vietnam hawk who was so lonely and penniless that he became a Mafia puppet, begging mobsters for both cash and 'abortion advice' (as if the womanising Kennedy, with his family's $400 million fortune, needed either). These stories are often peddled by authors or publishers with an axe to grind (in the US, remember, the CIA had some 40 'agent-journalists' on its payroll not that long ago – I doubt they've all gracefully taken early retirement).

JFK, MLK, RFK and John Lennon were all flawed men. But they cannot sue anybody now. They're sitting ducks. That doesn't mean we have to believe or encourage every foul 'revelation' – nor should we ever stop questioning the source or provenance of such attacks (in the UK, for instance, when Fenton Bresler's *Who Killed John Lennon?* was initially published – the first book to seriously discuss the links between Lennon's death and US intelligence – it was hammered in the broadsheet newspapers by reviewer Miles Copeland, though what the review didn't tell the readers was that Copeland's father was actually one of the CIA's co-founders…).

In early 2003 the UK's BBC TV invited British viewers to vote for the Greatest Briton of all time. Millions of votes were cast over a period of months. The poll was topped, of course, by the original Winston – Britain's wartime leader Churchill – the man widely held to have delivered the nation from Hitler.

But to the astonishment of conservative critics – who'd envisaged a list that would be completely dominated by prime ministers, generals, scientists and royalty – John Lennon reached as high as Number Three before finally settling at Number Seven. Not bad for a rock 'n' roller who'd not been in cynical Britain for over three decades, a 'nowhere man' who'd been dead for some 23 years.

A blue plaque – for 'JOHN LENNON 1940–1980 MUSICIAN & SONGWRITER' – was unveiled in April 2003 by Sir John Mills at the site of the old Apple boutique in London's Baker Street.

The event was attended by various celebrities including movie star Jean-Claude Van Damme, Liver Bird Nerys Hughes, singer Jess Conrad, dancer Lionel Blair, actress Anita Harris and John's old acting pal Victor Spinetti. The paparazzi were present, too, as were hundreds of fans, many of them smiling through their tears.

'He knew he meant a lot to people,' said May Pang the same month, '[but] I think he would have been astounded at how profoundly his death was felt throughout the world.'

A one-hour BBC TV show was dedicated to Lennon; it was narrated by actor Alan Davies who'd flown up to Liverpool's John Lennon International Airport. It was broadcast a couple of months before a remix of Yoko Ono's 'Walking On Thin Ice' reached Number One in the US dance charts, just as Lennon had said it would during the very last afternoon of his life…

It was some 18 years after his assassination that a John Lennon box set, *The Lennon Anthology*, was released. This EMI issue contained 94 tracks, many of them out-takes, spread across four CDs. There was a 64-page booklet too. In the latter Yoko described Lennon as a 'heavy dude', someone who was a 'king' not a mere pop prince. She also, poignantly, included the open letter to New York – and the world – which the pair of them had sent to *The New York Times* in May 1979 at the height of Lennon's hermit-like 'retirement'.

It was the note that, for all its mystical isolation, contained the first hints that Lennon was not just watching the wheels go round – the first signs of his explosive comeback, the comeback that was to be cut short, the comeback that was to prove to have such fatal consequences: 'We understand that, we, the city, the country, the earth are facing very hard times…the future of the earth is up to all of us…everybody is asking us What, When and Why…'.

The relationship that propelled Lennon into the avant-garde – and into prolonged political activism – had begun with a simple positive: the word 'Yes', which Yoko Ono had taped to the ceiling of London's Indica art gallery in 1966. The relationship ended – in the physical sense – some 14 years later with the same word, Lennon's last word before he was silenced. It was a faint answer to a cop's question, as he lay dying in the back of a NYPD police car, the same question that had ended 'Fame', the Bowie hit he'd co-written; 'What's your name? Are you John Lennon?' '…yes…'.

So it was perhaps appropriate that John and Yoko's May 1979 letter – while discussing angels and silence – should also end on a straightforward, positive note:

'remember, our silence is a silence of love and not of indifference. Remember, we are writing in the sky instead of on paper… Remember, we love you…'

Appendix

Lenono
Studio One
1 West 72nd Street
New York New York 10023

I told Sean what had happened. I showed him the picture of his father on the cover of the paper and explained the situation. I took Sean to the spot where John lay after he was shot. Sean wanted to know why the person shot John if he liked John. I explained that he was probably a confused person. Sean said we should find out if he was confused or if he really meant to kill John. I said that was up to the court. He asked what court – a tennis court or a basketball court? That's how he used to talk with his father. They were buddies. John would have been proud of Sean if he had heard this. Sean cried later. He also said 'Now Daddy is part of god. I guess when you die you become much more bigger because you're part of everything.'

I don't have much more to add to Sean's statement. The silent vigil will take place December 14th at 2pm for ten minutes.

Our thoughts will be with you.

Love
Yoko and Sean
Dec 10 '80, NYC

Discography

JOHN LENNON - SOLO UK HIT SINGLES

'Give Peace A Chance' (1969)
'Cold Turkey' (1969)
'Instant Karma' (1970)*
'Power To The People' (1971)*
'Happy Xmas! (War Is Over)' (1972)*
'Mind Games' (1973)
'Whatever Gets You Through The Night' (1974)*
'Number 9 Dream' (1975)
'Stand By Me' (1975)
'Imagine' (1975)
'(Just Like) Starting Over' (1980)
'Woman' (1981)
'Watching The Wheels' (1981)
'Love' (1982)
'Nobody Told Me' (1984)
'Borrowed Time' (1984)
'Jealous Guy' (1985)
* *with the Plastic Ono Band and others*

JOHN LENNON - SOLO UK HIT ALBUMS

John Lennon & The Plastic Ono Band (1971)*
Imagine (1971)*

Sometime In New York City (1972)*
Mind Games (1973)
Walls And Bridges (1974)
Rock 'n' Roll (1975)
Shaved Fish (1975)
Double Fantasy (1980)**
The John Lennon Collection (1981)
Milk And Honey (1984)**
Live In New York City (1986)
Imagine – Music From The Motion Picture (1988)***
* *with the Plastic Ono Band and others*
** *with Yoko Ono*
*** *with some tracks by The Beatles*

THE 1980 BERMUDA AND HIT FACTORY SESSIONS

Recorded: Bermuda 22 June–27 July
Hit Factory 7 August–10 September
(although versions of most of the following are on *Double Fantasy* and *Milk And Honey*, in their entirety they're only currently available as the rare *Heartplay Parts 1 and 2* CD bootleg; times and titles may vary slightly)

Track 1. I'm Steppin' Out
4 mins 59 secs – stereo
A spirited, driving – and technically clean version. An arrangement inspired by a June night in Bermuda's Flavours nightclub where Lennon had heard the B-52s 'Rock Lobster' for the first time and found it, like certain Lene Lovich tracks, comparable with sounds Yoko had been making ten years before (as with the new wave in general, and The Clash in particular, Lennon became something of a B-52s fan during the last summer of his life).

'Rock Lobster' also convinced him that he was on the right track, that a true 50/50 album with Yoko would bring out the best in both of them (in the morning he recorded the first version – confusingly it's down as take 2).

Starts with a fade-in and John's ironic ad-lib:

'… well, he finally gets the kid to bed and he goes into his *own* space – and this is how it goes!'.

After a few ad-libs 'begin the beguine!' and a few too many 'screw it!' comments, it ends with a great, jagged guitar riff and a slightly hoarse Lennon asking for more volume in his headphones 'more voice so I don't have to break my balls…'.

Track 2. I'm Losing You

4 mins 17 secs – stereo

Written after Lennon had been unable to get Yoko on the phone. Contains some great, howling guitar just before the fade.

Track 3. Clean Up Time

2 mins 23 secs – stereo

Jokey, very early version with the song only half arranged. Complete with some chat with guitarist Earl Slick and a parody of French rap. Short but fascinating in that you can hear the foundations falling into space.

Track 4. Clean Up Time (take 2)

4 mins 24 secs – stereo

A smoother, more complete effort, with silken vocals from Lennon, much pounding piano and some heavy drum touches.

Track 5. Clean Up Time (take 3)

3 mins 23 secs – stereo

Although there's a little hiss – and some deliberate, sometimes very effective, overdubbing of children's laughter – this is the closest of the first three takes to a 'proper' track.

Track 6. (Just Like) Starting Over (intro)

2 mins 28 secs – stereo demo

> 'It's been s'long since we bin apart,
>
> Me feet are hurtin' and I start to fart!'

A long mucking-around intro to Lennon's affectionate '50s parody, with much arrangement chat and some funky Earl Slick gee-tar.

JL: 'That's lovely bass! I love it! They didn't have that in those days, that's the only thing they didn't have – that's a good bass... Hugh get on the 'phones then you wouldn't play so f—ing loud.'

Hugh McCracken: 'I can't hear ya, I don't have my 'phones on!'

Engineer: We're rolling.

JL: [OTT showbiz voice] '... this one's for Gene and Eddie and Elvis – and Buddy...'

Track 7. (Just Like) Starting Over

4 mins 9 secs – stereo

Some slight background hiss doesn't hide the fact Lennon's in fine voice here with a version that, despite some distorted guitar, seems a little lighter on its feet than the official release.

JL: 'I love it... OK, if that's it, let's hear it again.'

Track 8. Beautiful Boy

4 mins 5 secs – stereo

A heartbreakingly pure take – made poignantly better, or worse, by some end dialogue with young Sean.

Track 9. Dear Yoko

3 mins 14 secs – stereo

Some heavy slap-back echo on Lennon's vocal here, almost Johnny Burnette Trio territory. It starts with a ridiculous parody – three-quarters upper-class English toff (a fop Winston Churchill?) with an end dash of Groucho Marx – before slipping into some dodgy arrangement chat.

JL: 'Remember the intro, I'll get in somewhere there, y'know, as long as you leave a hole I can get huh-huh. And if I don't get it...'

Engineer: 'But where is the hole?'

JL: 'The hole's where you feel it.'

Track 10. Watching The Wheels
3 mins 33 secs – stereo
An uneven lacklustre mix, with the electric piano overly loud, which still sounds listenable – but that might just be down to the sheer quality of the song.

Track 11. I Am The Walrus
0 mins 14 secs – stereo
> 'I am he as you are he,
> as we are thee and you are all together,
> Boo boo boo boo boo,
> See how they run like pigs in a gu...'

JL: [laughs] 'I mean the whole f—in' thing was like that.'
A smiling look back at The Beatles.

Track 12. Woman (intro)
2 mins 6 secs – stereo
JL: [arch voice] 'I love double tracking!... when we first discovered it I double-tracked everything. On the second album was when he suddenly told us that you could do this thing, y'know. I wouldn't let him have anything single track from then on. He'd say [desperate voice] "Please, just leave this one." No! [wheezy chuckle]... "Woman, I know your underpants"... I still feel like I'm in the f—ing Beatles with this track!'
Engineer: 'OK, can we let it roll 'cos I'm keepin' this – '
JL: 'Mmm, I just we should have started going [sharp intake of breath] turn it into "Girl" [laughs]...[High *a capella* chorus of 'Woman']
Yoko: 'You sound like a Beatle!'
JL: [mock anger] 'An Ex-Beatle You F—ing F—! [laughs] Actually I'm s'posed to be Smokey Robinson at the moment, my dear. (The Beatles were always supposing they were Smokey Robinson.) Because... can I have the guitar in my ears? ... one of my ears anyway... Arthur, this is early motown-Beatles, circa '64, ballad. Huh-huh. That's how I think of it in my head, anyway... OK, hello? Hello? Can we hear something round here? Ah, thank you. OK, guys, let's lay down and sing to your mother or sister or anybody that's of the female race 'cos

that's who you're playing to...it's only the guys who like that heavy shit... 1–2–3–'

Track 13. Woman

3 mins 19 secs – stereo
Starts with the 'Four!' from the intro take's tail then, as you'd expect, goes straight into a gentle, piano-led version of a Lennon classic.

Track 14. Dream Lover / Stay

3 mins 41 secs – stereo
'... Dream lover, where are you? Up my ass and in the stew!'
Bobby Darin was never like this! Take out the smut, though, and this pushing rocker would be great heads-down cover. Are those FX guitar pedals or just track overspill? After hitting the three-minute mark JL slips into Maurice Williams' 'Stay'.

Track 15. Forgive Me, My Little Flower Princess

3 mins 37 secs – stereo
Recorded on 14 August. A touching light 'n' breezy piece of semi-acoustic soul that, lyrically at least, is thought to have been aimed at Yoko Ono (though some believe it is also aimed at May Pang). Overtones of the Isley Brothers at their best – the Isleys and what might have been... at the end Lennon tries to cheer himself up.
JL: [toff idiot] 'It almost had my foot tapping...'

Track 16. Nobody Told Me

3 mins 50 secs – stereo
Another light-hearted run-through...
'Nazis in the bathroom' indeed. Most peculiar, Mother.

Track 17. I Don't Wanna Face It

2 mins 33 secs – stereo
'Ein! Schwi! Hickle! Fickle!'
Has a wonderful gee-tar break of jagged delirium around the one and half minute mark. Short, sharp and bitter-sweet.

Track 18. Borrowed Time

4 mins 4 secs – stereo

Begins with someone else's dub cut then shifts into a softer reggae mould. Ends with Lennon telling us, in a bizarre Jamaican accent, how 'it got me quite worried. But I don't take it so seriously, I don't take it at all, in fact. I gave it up!'

Track 19. Woman (take 2)

3 mins 39 secs – stereo

Dedicated to the other half 'of the sky'. The added female backing vocals, give it a pleasing texture. Fades on the word 'forever…'

Track 20. The Great Wok

2 mins 3 secs – stereo

An amusing, at times hilarious, monologue from a long-lost Indian guru who's prepared to give up everything except complete luxury.

Track 21. Watching The Wheels (take 2)

1 min 57 secs – stereo

A slow piano blues spin on the 'hermit epic'. Flawed but magical.

Track 22. Watching The Wheels (take 3)

3 mins 41 secs – stereo

Rock 'n' roll 12-bar holler – harshly recorded and with vocals that vary between the soulful and a pop WC Fields.

Track 23. Watching The Wheels (take 4)

2 mins 48 secs – mono

Very close to take 3 – apart from the Captain And Tennille ad-libs. 'We've reversed ourselves but we don't care.'

Track 24. Corinna Corinna

1 min 15 secs – stereo

The golden oldie gets taken for a walk.

Track 25. Watching The Wheels (take 5)

2 mins 59 secs – stereo

'Watching...' as Robert Zimmerman would have done it, with the acoustic guitar really singing out. (Though I doubt if Dylan would have had mic pops or Yoko muttering quietly on the left channel but, hey, who can tell?) Pretty damn good, all in all.

Track 26. I Don't Wanna Face It (take 2)

0 mins 43 secs – stereo

Acoustic, and done with an OTT hillbilly accent.

Track 27. Welcome To Bermuda

0 mins 9 secs – stereo

Sounds like the Wok.

Track 28. I Don't Wanna Face It (take 3)

2 mins 3 secs – stereo

Singing against himself with a bit of natural double tracking.

Track 29. Woman (take 3)

3 mins 6 secs – stereo

Slow, poorly recorded shot – despite being the 'third take' in terms of running order, this is almost certainly the first. As with the 'Dylan version' of 'Watching...', it does, for all its weaknesses, show the strength of the basic original arrangement.

Track 30. I'm Steppin' Out (take 2)

4 mins 32 secs – stereo

Crude, drum machine version – the very first.

Track 31. Nobody Told Me (take 2)

2 mins 21 secs – stereo

Crude, drum machine version – piano's so bad it's actually good.

Track 32. Nobody Told Me (take 3)
3 mins 11 secs – stereo
Slightly better drum machine version – dedicated to Ringo (who else?).

Track 33. Beautiful Boy (take 2)
2 mins 35 secs – stereo
Crude drum machine version complete with handclaps.

Track 34. Borrowed Time (take 2)
3 mins 43 secs – stereo
Soulful but basic take.

Track 35. Dear Yoko (take 2)
3 mins 35 secs – stereo
Again, confusingly, this acoustic take-two version – with somebody's fingerpops in the background – is actually the first one. Lennon's vocals are full of yearning.

Track 36. Too Much Monkey Business
1 min 17 secs – stereo
Rock 'n' roll gem gets the Lennon-as-Dylan treatment.

Track 37. Clean-Up Time (take 4)
2 mins 40 secs – stereo
Piano and keyboard version.

Track 38. I'm Losing You (take 2)
3 mins 17 secs – stereo
Piano blues version (with touches of the Lennon-McCartney 'You Never Give Me Your Money'). Probably the original version. Lennon virtually alone and at his most vulnerable.

Track 39. I'm Losing You (take 3 – abridged)
1 min 30 secs – stereo
Piano blues version, cut short by a fast fade.

Track 40. I'm Losing You (take 4 – abridged)
1 min 41 secs – stereo
Drum machine version, cut short by a fade.

Track 41. Howling At The Moon
1 min 56 secs – stereo
Drum machine version.

Track 42. I'm A Man
1 min 51 secs – stereo
Howling Wolf meets Louis Armstrong acoustic version of the much-covered blues gem.

Track 43. I Watch Your Face
1 min 10 secs – stereo
Cassette-quality acoustic demo.

Track 44. Losing You
2 mins 32 secs – stereo
Cassette-quality acoustic demo.

Track 45. (Just Like) Starting Over (take 2)
1 min 36 secs – stereo
A bitter, piano version with Lennon griping at the outside world ('...we can't fill your empty lives for you...').

Track 46. (Just Like) Starting Over (take 3)
2 mins 10 secs – stereo
Spaced-out, drum machine version.

Track 47. (Just Like) Starting Over (take 4)
4 mins 53 secs – stereo
Guitar and drum machine version. Throbs along nicely ('... the time has come,' the Walrus said, 'for you and me to stay in bed – again...').

Track 48. That Was A Nice Noise

2 mins 23 secs – stereo

Lennon's parody of a hillbilly folkie gives way to 20 seconds of silence and then a 1 to 12 countdown by young Sean Lennon – who then adds some sweet guitar cacophony, 'I like it loud!' says the youngster before his father ends it by saying the title.

JOHN LENNON'S BEATLES SONGS

The following Beatles singles were mostly, or wholly, written by John Lennon.

'Please Please Me'
'Ask Me Why'
'Thank You Girl'
'I'll Get You'
'I Want To Hold Your Hand'
'You Can't Do That'
'A Hard Day's Night'
'She's A Woman'
'Ticket To Ride'
'Help!'
'Day Tripper'
'Rain'
'Strawberry Fields Forever'
'All You Need Is Love'
'I Am The Walrus'
'Lady Madonna'
'Revolution'
'Don't Let Me Down'
'Ballad Of John And Yoko'
'Come Together'
'You Know My Name (Look Up The Number)'

The following Beatles album tracks were mostly, or wholly, written by John Lennon.

'Misery'
'There's A Place'
'It Won't Be Long'
'Little Child'
'Not A Second Time'
'If I Fell'
'Any Time At All'
'I'll Cry Instead'
'When I Get Home'
'You Can't Do That'
'No Reply'
'I'm A Loser'
'Baby's In Black'
'Eight Days A Week'
'The Night Before'
'You're Gonna Lose That Girl'
'It's Only Love'
'Tell Me What You See'
'Norwegian Wood'
'Nowhere Man'
'The Word'
'I'm Looking Through You'
'In My Life'
'Run For Your Life'
'I'm Only Sleeping'
'She Said, She Said'
'And Your Bird Can Sing'
'Doctor Robert'
'Tomorrow Never Knows'
'Lucy In The Sky With Diamonds'
'Fixing A Hole'
'Benefit Of Mr Kite!'

'A Day In The Life'
'Dear Prudence'
'Glass Onion'
'Wild Honey Pie'
'Bungalow Bill'
'Happiness Is A Warm Gun'
'I'm So Tired'
'Why Don't We Do It In The Road'
'Julia'
'Everybody's Got Something To Hide Except For Me And My Monkey'
'Sexy Sadie'
'Revolution 9'
'Cry Baby Cry'
'All Together Now'
'Hey Bulldog'
'I Want You (She's So Heavy)'
'Mean Mr Mustard'
'Polythene Pam'
'Carry That Weight'
'Two Of Us'
'Dig A Pony'
'Across The Universe'
'Dig It'
'The One After 909'

John Lennon's Number Nine List

John Lennon was born at 6:30pm on 9 October 1940 and at school he sat, and subsequently failed, 9 GCE 'O' Level exams while the bus he caught daily to art college was No 72 (seven plus two making nine).

The registration number of the car that killed his mother was LKF630 (six plus three equalling nine). The car was driven by a Merseyside policeman, his force number being PC126 (one plus two plus six).

John's first group was The Quarrymen (nine letters), Penny Lane (nine letters) is in postal district 18 (two times nine) of the Liverpool 9 area and he met his first wife Cynthia when she was still living at 18 Trinity Road, Holylake.

His first son, Julian Lennon, was born at Sefton Green General Hospital, Liverpool which is situated at 126 Smithdown Road (which was also the medical institute where John's stepfather and mother were both pronounced dead).

Brian Epstein first saw The Beatles at the Cavern club on 9 November 1961 and he later managed to secure The Beatles an EMI recording deal on 9 May 1962.

'Love Me Do', their debut, was a Parlophone release with the matrix number R4949.

'She Loves You', 'Can't Buy Me Love', 'Day Tripper', 'We Can Work It Out', 'Give Peace A Chance' and 'Happy Xmas! (War Is Over)' were all singles that charted in the UK on the ninth day of the month. The Beatles created a record TV audience of 73 million in the USA on their *Ed Sullivan Show* debut dated 9 February 1964.

Lennon first met Yoko Ono on 9 November 1966 and when he

married her – and she became Yoko Ono Lennon and he became John Ono Lennon – they had a total of nine Os in their combined names.

Other key figures in his life had nine letters in their names – like John's aunt Mimi Smith, Jim Gretty who sold him his first guitar, Bill Harry of *Merseybeat* magazine, and Bob Wooler and Liz Hughes of the Cavern. Perhaps the two most influential people in terms of his early artistic career – the art college Dean Stevenson and John's friend and co-composer Paul McCartney – both had nine letters in their surnames.

John wrote the songs 'Revolution 9', 'No 9 Dream' – which then reached Number Nine in the charts – and 'The One After 909' (the latter was said to have been written at mother Julia's house, 9 Newcastle Road, Liverpool) and he would sometimes joke that the greatest song he'd probably ever written, the anthemic 'All You Need Is Love', had a nine-word chorus.

He later sold Tittenhurst Park to Ringo Starr on 9 September 1973 and, later that year, whenever John gambled on the roulette wheel in Las Vegas, he would always bet on number nine (where he always lost every penny).

Yoko Ono lived at West 72nd Street NYC and later their Dakota apartment number was 72. At this time he also released *Walls And Bridges*, with its cover being a Lennon painting of himself, aged 11, showing a footballer with large number nine on his shirt.

The release of *Walls And Bridges* came nine years after The Beatles' debut in Paris. That day, a few hours before the gig, John had received a neatly typed note – it contained just nine words: 'I Am Going To Shoot You At Nine Tonight'...

And, of course, as noted above, it was 9 December in Britain when John Lennon was shot dead...

The Last Will And Testament Of John Winston Ono Lennon

I, JOHN WINSTON ONO LENNON, a resident of the County of New York, State of New York, which I declare to be my domicile do hereby make, publish and declare this to be my Last Will and Testament, hereby revoking all other Wills, Codicils and Testamentary dispositions by me at any time heretofore made.

FIRST: The expenses of my funeral and the administration of my estate, and all inheritance, estate or succession taxes, including interest and penalties, payable by reason of my death shall be paid out of and charged generally against the principal of my residuary estate without apportionment or proration. My executor shall not seek contribution or reimbursement for any such payments.

SECOND: Should my wife survive me, I give, devise and bequeath to her absolutely, an amount equal to that portion of my residuary estate, the numerator and denominator of which shall be determined as follows:

1. The numerator shall be an amount equal to one-half (½) of my adjusted gross estate less the value of all other property included in my gross estate for Federal Estate Tax purposes and which pass or shall have passed to my wife either under any other provision of this Will or in any manner outside of this Will in such manner as to qualify for and be allowed as a marital deduction. The words 'pass', 'have passed', 'marital deduction' and 'adjusted gross estate' shall have the same meaning as said words have under those provisions of the United States Internal Revenue Code applicable to my estate.

2. The denominator shall be an amount representing the value of my residuary estate.

THIRD: I give, devise and bequeath all the rest, residue and remainder of my estate, wheresoever situate, to the Trustees under a Trust Agreement dated November 12, 1979, which I signed with my wife YOKO ONO, and ELI GARBER as Trustees, to be added to the trust property and held and distributed in accordance with the terms of that agreement and any amendments made pursuant to its terms before my death.

FOURTH: In the event that my wife and I die under such circumstances that there is not sufficient evidence to determine which of us has predeceased the other, I hereby declare it to be my will that it shall be deemed that I shall have predeceased her and that this, my Will, and any and all of its provisions shall be construed based upon that assumption.

FIFTH: I hereby nominate, constitute and appoint my beloved wife YOKO ONO, to act as the Executor of this my Last Will and Testament. In the event that my beloved wife YOKO ONO shall predecease me or chooses not to act for any reason, I nominate and appoint ELI GARBER, DAVID WARMFLASH and CHARLES PETTIT, in the order named, to act in her place and stead.

SIXTH: I shall nominate, constitute and appoint my wife YOKO ONO, as the Gurdian [sic] of the person and property of any children of the marriage who may survive me. In the event that she predeceases me, or for any reason she chooses not to act in that capacity, I nominate constitute and appoint SAM GREEN to act in her place and stead.

SEVENTH: No person named herein to serve in any fiduciary capacity shall be required to file or post any bond for the faithful performance of his or her duties, in that capacity in this or in any other jurisdiction, any law to the contrary not withstanding.

EIGHTH: If any legatee or beneficiary under this will or the trust agreement between myself as Grantor and YOKO ONO LENNON and ELI GARBER as Trustees, dated November 12, 1979 shall interpose objections to the probate of this Will,or institute or prosecute or be in any way interested or instrumental in the institution or prosecution of any action or proceeding for the purpose of setting aside or invalidating this Will, then and in each such case, I direct that such legatee or beneficiary shall receive nothing whatsoever under this Will or the aforementioned Trust.

IN WITNESS THEREOF, I have subscribed and sealed and do publish and declare these presents as and for my Last Will and Testament, this 12th day of November, 1979.

[signed] John Lennon

Index